To the ancient sages and seers of India, who through their wisdom and insight, have illuminated the path to self-discovery and enlightenment for countless generations.

To the great texts of Indian philosophy and spirituality, such as the Vedas, Upanishads, and Bhagavad Gita, which have served as a source of inspiration and guidance for so many.

To the teachers and practitioners of Indian spiritual traditions, who have dedicated their lives to preserving and sharing this wisdom with others.

And to all those who seek to deepen their understanding of themselves and the world around them, may the wisdom of ancient India continue to guide and inspire you on your journey.

This book is a humble attempt to share some of the timeless wisdom of ancient India and pay a tribute to ancient knowledge. May this book be a small step in spreading the light of ancient knowledge to all corners of the world.

WISDOM OF LOST BHARAT

REDISCOVERING THE ANCIENT PATH TO ENLIGHTENMENT

CHINTAN AGGARWAL

Contents

Contents

Contents

Contents

Contents

Preface

The ancient wisdom of India has been a source of inspiration and guidance for generations. From the profound insights of the Vedas and Upanishads, to the ethical teachings of the Bhagavad Gita, these texts have shaped the spiritual and philosophical landscape of India for centuries. They offer a wealth of knowledge on the nature of reality, the purpose of life, and the path to enlightenment.

This book is an attempt to share some of this ancient wisdom with a wider audience. It is a collection of selected teachings and insights from Indian philosophy and spirituality, presented in a way that is accessible and relevant to modern readers. Whether you are a spiritual seeker, a student of philosophy, or simply someone who is curious about the ancient wisdom of India, this book has something to offer.

In this book, we explore the fundamental principles of Indian spirituality and philosophy, including the concept of karma, the nature of the self, and the path to liberation. We also delve into the teachings of some of India's most revered texts, such as the Vedas, Upanishads, and Bhagavad Gita, drawing out their key insights and teachings.

It is my hope that this book will serve as a valuable resource for those interested in exploring the ancient wisdom of India. May it inspire you to delve deeper into the rich and profound teachings of this great tradition, and may it help guide you on your own journey of self-discovery and enlightenment.

Acknowledgements

Writing a book on the ancient wisdom of India is a humbling experience, and I am deeply grateful to all those who have helped me along the way.

First and foremost, I would like to thank the ancient sages and seers of India, whose wisdom and insight have been the foundation of this book. Their teachings continue to inspire and guide people across the world, and I am honored to have had the opportunity to share some of their wisdom in this book.

I would also like to thank the many scholars, teachers, and practitioners of Indian spirituality and philosophy who have dedicated their lives to preserving and sharing this wisdom. Their work has been an invaluable resource for me, and I have greatly benefited from their scholarship and teachings.

I am also deeply grateful to my editor and publisher for their guidance, support, and encouragement throughout the writing process. Without their help, this book would not have been possible.

Lastly, I would like to thank my family and friends for their love and support. Their unwavering encouragement and belief in me has been a constant source of inspiration throughout the writing of this book.

This book is a small tribute to the ancient knowledge and wisdom of India, and I am honored to have had the opportunity to share it with others.

1. The Philosophy of Bhārat

The philosophy of Bhārat is an ancient system of thought and spiritual practice originating from the Indian subcontinent. It is based on the concept of Dharma, or righteousness, which is the foundation for living a righteous and fulfilling life. The power of action, non-action, and will are important aspects of Dharma. The Law of Karma states that for every action, there is a consequence. This law also emphasizes the unity of existence and the power of interconnectedness between all beings. Devotion to spiritual practices is seen as the path to self-realization and enlightenment. Silence, meditation, and other forms of introspection can help one to understand the nature of consciousness and one's true self. Ultimately, the path of liberation and inner peace is found through the practice of these teachings.

CHAPTER I

The Concept of Dharma

Dharma is an ancient Indian term that encompasses a wide range of meanings, but is most commonly defined as a religious and moral code of conduct that applies to all aspects of life. The concept of Dharma has been an integral part of Indian society and culture for thousands of years and is still widely practiced today. The concept of Dharma is closely related to the notion of karma, or the law of cause and effect. According to ancient Hindu texts, the performance of one's Dharma is the most important factor in determining one's destiny.

The concept of Dharma is rooted in the Vedic tradition, which is the oldest and most authoritative of the four branches of Hinduism. The Vedas are a collection of sacred texts that contain the teachings of the ancient sages and are believed to be divinely revealed. The Vedas emphasize the need for righteous living and for individuals to fulfill their Dharma, or religious and moral duties. The Vedas also provide guidance on how to live a just and virtuous life.

The concept of Dharma is closely linked to the idea of karma. Dharma refers to the duties, obligations and responsibilities of an individual, while karma refers to the consequences of one's actions. According to the Vedas, the performance of one's Dharma is essential for spiritual growth and the attainment of moksha, or liberation from the cycle of birth and death. The performance of Dharma also helps to create balance and harmony in the world.

The concept of Dharma has been further developed in the Bhagavad Gita, a sacred Hindu text. In the Bhagavad

Gita, Krishna explains to Arjuna the importance of Dharma. He explains that Dharma is the foundation of a just and virtuous life, and that it is essential for individuals to fulfill their Dharma in order to achieve moksha.

The concept of Dharma is also central to the teachings of Buddhism. The Buddha taught his followers to follow the Eightfold Path, which consists of right understanding, right thought, right speech, right action, right livelihood, right effort, right mindfulness, and right concentration. These eight elements of the Eightfold Path are all based on the concept of Dharma and are meant to guide the individual on the path to enlightenment.

The concept of Dharma is also closely linked to the concept of Ahimsa, or nonviolence. Ahimsa is the practice of nonviolence towards all living beings, including animals and plants. The practice of Ahimsa is closely connected to the performance of Dharma, as it is believed that by practicing Ahimsa one is able to create a more harmonious and peaceful world.

The concept of Dharma is an ancient and profound one. It is a code of conduct that guides individuals on their spiritual journey and helps them to lead a life of service and justice. The performance of Dharma is essential for the attainment of moksha and for the creation of a harmonious and peaceful world. The concept of Dharma is an integral part of the ancient wisdom of Bharat and is still widely practiced today.

CHAPTER II

The Power of Action

The Power of Action is a concept that has been discussed for centuries by philosophers, religious leaders, and modern-day thinkers alike. It refers to the notion that taking action is more powerful than simply thinking or planning. This idea can be seen throughout our lives—from the smallest decisions to the grandest goals—and has been a cornerstone of many great civilizations, including the ancient Indian culture of Bharat.

Action is often seen as the key to success in many areas of life. By taking action, we can create the future we desire, rather than merely relying on luck or fate. It is through action that we can make our dreams a reality, while still accounting for any possible challenges that may arise. Action is also essential in order to make sure that our plans are actually put into practice. Without action, plans remain unfulfilled and dreams remain just that—dreams.

The ancient Bharat civilization held the power of action in high regard. In fact, the Rig Veda, one of the oldest known religious texts, speaks of the importance of action in achieving success. The Vedic texts stress the importance of exerting effort and perseverance in order to achieve any goal. This idea is echoed in the works of the great Hindu philosopher, Patanjali, who wrote about the power of action in his famous treatise, the Yoga Sutras.

The ancient Bharat civilization also valued the power of action in acquiring knowledge. In the Upanishads, the ancient texts of Hindu philosophy, it is stated that knowledge can be acquired only through action. This means that knowledge is not something that can be attained through thought alone; it must be sought after through action.

The power of action has also been an important theme in Buddhism. The teachings of the Buddha stress the importance of taking action in order to attain enlightenment. The Buddha himself was a great proponent of the power of action, and his teachings serve as an example of how action can be used to pursue one's goals.

The power of action is a powerful concept that has been embraced by many cultures throughout history. In Bharat, action has been seen as an essential tool for achieving success, acquiring knowledge, and attaining enlightenment. By taking action, we can make our dreams a reality and overcome any obstacle that may arise. In taking action, we can create our own destiny, rather than relying on luck or fate. The power of action is a timeless concept that can help us to achieve our goals and live our lives to the fullest.

CHAPTER III

The Power of Non-Action

The Power of Non-Action has been a concept of great importance to many ancient cultures and philosophies, including that of the lost Bharat. Non-action, also known as wu-wei, is a concept that emphasizes the importance of action without exerting too much effort in achieving one's goals. This concept is based on the belief that there is a natural way of doing things and that the most effective action is to just let things happen without trying to control the outcome.

Non-action can be seen as a way to achieve balance and harmony in life. It is a way to let go and trust in the natural unfolding of events. This approach is one of acceptance and allowing, as opposed to trying to control and manipulate the outcome. It is about letting go of attachment to the outcome and allowing for the natural process to take its course.

The concept of non-action is deeply rooted in the ancient wisdom of the lost Bharat. In the Upanishads, a collection of ancient Hindu scriptures, non-action is seen as the highest form of action. The Upanishads state that a person who is able to act without any attachment to the outcome will experience true inner peace and harmony. The Bhagavad Gita, another ancient Hindu scripture, also speaks of non-action as a way to achieve inner peace and freedom from suffering.

The concept of non-action is also found in the teachings of the Buddha. The Buddha taught that attachment to outcomes leads to suffering. He taught that the most skillful way to act is to be mindful and live in the present moment without clinging to the results of one's actions. This is a way to achieve inner peace and to be liberated from suffering.

The power of non-action is an important part of the ancient wisdom of the lost Bharat. It is a way to find balance and harmony in life, to let go of attachments and to trust in the natural unfolding of events. It is a way to achieve inner peace and freedom from suffering. By letting go and accepting the natural process, we can be liberated from the cycle of suffering and find true inner peace.

CHAPTER IV

The Law of Karma

The Law of Karma, also known as the law of cause and effect, is an ancient spiritual belief that has been passed down through generations since the time of the Vedas—the oldest Hindu scriptures. This law states that every action has a reaction and that our actions have consequences in both this life and the next. In Hinduism, the concept of reincarnation is closely tied to the law of karma—the belief that our actions in this life can determine our fate in future lives.

Karma is an important part of Hinduism and Buddhism, and it is one of the main beliefs that unites these two religions. According to the law of karma, our actions in this life set in motion a chain of causes and effects that will determine our future. This means that if we act with kindness and compassion, we will reap the consequences of our actions in a positive way. Conversely, if we act with cruelty and selfishness, we will suffer the consequences in a negative way.

The law of karma is based on the idea that our actions have an effect on the world around us. Our thoughts and deeds can have a ripple effect on the universe, creating a cycle of positive and negative energy. This law teaches us that we are responsible for our own actions and that we should act in a way that will bring positive results. If we treat others with respect and compassion, our kindness will be repaid with kindness. If we act with malice and selfishness, our actions will create negative consequences for us.

The concept of karma is closely related to the idea of reincarnation in Hinduism and Buddhism. According to this belief, when we die, our souls are reborn in a new body and our karma from previous lives can influence our circumstances in this life. In other words, the actions we take in this life will determine our fate in our next life.

The law of karma teaches us to live our lives with integrity and to take responsibility for our actions. It is a reminder that our actions have consequences and that we should strive to act in a way that will bring us positive results. The law of karma is a powerful spiritual teaching that can help us to lead our lives with purpose and intention. By following the law of karma, we can strive to create a better world for ourselves and future generations.

CHAPTER V

The Unity of Existence

The Unity of Existence is an ancient philosophical concept that has been discussed and explored by thinkers throughout the ages. It is a central theme in Hinduism, Jainism, Buddhism, Sikhism, and Taoism, and is also found in Western philosophies such as Neoplatonism, Gnosticism, and Hermeticism. In its most basic definition, the Unity of Existence is the recognition that all beings – from the smallest atom to the largest star – are interconnected, forming a single, unified Whole.

Understanding the Unity of Existence is essential for understanding the relationship between individuals and their environment, as well as the relationship between the individual and the Divine. According to this view, every aspect of existence is part of a larger, all-encompassing unity – nothing exists in isolation. We are all connected, and our actions have consequences that ripple out through the universe. This interconnectedness is the basis for compassion, morality, and ethics.

The Unity of Existence is a central theme in the ancient wisdom of Bharat (India). In the Upanishads, one of the most important ancient texts of India, this concept is explored in great detail. According to the Upanishads, the entire Universe is a single, unified, indivisible consciousness. This consciousness is the ultimate source of all life and the ultimate truth. All the different aspects of existence – from material objects to the subtlest spiritual planes – are merely different manifestations of this all-encompassing unity.

The Bhagavad Gita, another ancient text of India, also emphasizes the importance of the Unity of Existence. In this text, Krishna, the Supreme Being, explains that all living beings are connected. He states that all beings are equal and share a single, indivisible existence. Therefore, all beings should be treated with respect and compassion.

The Unity of Existence was also an important theme in the ancient wisdom of the Upanishads and the Bhagavad Gita. According to this view, all existence is interconnected, and this interconnectedness is the source of compassion and morality. This concept of Unity of Existence is essential for understanding the relationship between individuals and their environment, as well as the relationship between the individual and the Divine.

The Unity of Existence is a central theme in many of the spiritual practices of India. Yoga, for example, is said to bring about a deep understanding of the oneness of all existence. Similarly, meditation is said to bring about a sense of unity with all of existence. This is why meditation is so important in Hinduism and other Indian spiritual traditions.

The Unity of Existence is also a major theme in the ancient wisdom of Bharat. In the Upanishads, for example, we are told that all existence is interconnected, and that there is a single, indivisible consciousness at the root of all existence. This is why it is so important to treat all beings with respect and compassion. Similarly, in the Bhagavad Gita, we are told that all living beings are equal and share a single, indivisible existence. Therefore, we should treat all beings with respect and compassion.

The Unity of Existence is a concept that has been explored and discussed by thinkers throughout the ages. It is a central theme in Hinduism, Jainism, Buddhism,

Sikhism, and Taoism, and is also found in Western philosophies such as Neoplatonism, Gnosticism, and Hermeticism. In its most basic definition, the Unity of Existence is the recognition that all beings – from the smallest atom to the largest star – are interconnected, forming a single, unified Whole. Understanding the Unity of Existence is essential for understanding the relationship between individuals and their environment, as well as the relationship between the individual and the Divine.

CHAPTER VI

The Power of Will

The Power of Will is a concept that has been talked about and studied in many cultures, religions, and philosophies. It is a concept that has been associated with success, happiness, and even personal transformation. In the ancient Indian culture of Bharat, the power of will was highly valued and was seen as essential for achieving one's goals and living a fulfilled life.

The power of will is often described as the ability to direct one's mental and physical energies toward a desired outcome. It is a skill that requires focus and discipline, as well as the capacity to remain motivated and determined no matter what the circumstances. In Bharat, this skill was seen as being essential for success in any endeavor, and was a cornerstone of the culture's teachings.

In the ancient texts of Bharat, the power of will was seen as a fundamental component of success, and the importance of cultivating it was stressed. For example, the Mahabharata states that "One must always strive to develop and strengthen the power of will. One must never give up, no matter how difficult the circumstances may be." This sentiment was echoed throughout the culture's teachings, with many other texts emphasizing the importance of maintaining a strong will and never giving up in the face of adversity.

The power of will was seen as a necessary component for spiritual growth and enlightenment as well. It was believed that by cultivating the power of will, an individual could transcend the physical and mental limitations of their body and mind, and access a higher level of consciousness. By doing so, it was believed that one could become more aware of the true nature of reality and cultivate a deeper understanding of the universe.

In Bharat, the power of will was also seen as an integral part of achieving success in any endeavor. It was believed that by cultivating the power of will, an individual could increase their chances of achieving their goals and dreams. Additionally, it was seen as a way to overcome obstacles and setbacks, and to remain focused and motivated even in difficult times.

The power of will was valued and celebrated in Bharat, with many of its teachings and practices dedicated to cultivating it. It was seen as a key component of personal growth, and many of its teachings focused on the importance of having a strong will. In addition, the culture placed a great emphasis on the importance of discipline and hard work, as it was believed that these two elements were essential for developing the power of will.

The power of will is still highly revered today and many of its teachings are still applicable to modern life. By cultivating the power of will, an individual can increase their chances of achieving success and living a fulfilled life. Additionally, the power of will can help an individual to remain focused and motivated even in difficult times, and to stay true to their goals and dreams. The wisdom of lost Bharat offers valuable insight into the power of will, and its teachings can still be applied today.

CHAPTER VII

The Path of Devotion

The Path of Devotion, or Bhakti Marga, is an ancient spiritual tradition that has been practiced in India for thousands of years. It is a path of love and devotion to God, which is expressed through prayer, meditation, and worship. The Path of Devotion is based on the belief that the ultimate source of happiness and fulfillment lies in connecting with the divine.

The path of devotion is rooted in the belief that all of creation is a manifestation of the divine, and that all beings are part of the same divine source. This understanding leads to a profound respect for life, and a deep sense of connectedness to the divine. Devotion involves surrendering to the divine, trusting in its will, and trusting in its grace.

The practice of devotion includes prayers, meditation, and worship. It also includes singing devotional songs, chanting mantras, and engaging in rituals such as puja. Through these activities, devotees seek to cultivate a deep connection with the divine.

The path of devotion is open to all, regardless of religion, caste, or any other social distinctions. It is a way of life that is both deeply personal and universal. It is a way of expressing love for the divine, and for all of life.

The goal of the path of devotion is to achieve a state of complete surrender to the divine, and to experience its love and grace. Devotion is a process of transformation, in which the devotee's ego is slowly dissolved and replaced by divine love. This brings about a profound sense of peace and joy.

The path of devotion is a journey of self-discovery, in which the devotee learns to recognize the divine within themselves and within all of life. It is a journey of love and surrender, and of finding joy in the simple things of life. Through devotion, devotees learn to appreciate the beauty and mystery of the divine and to become more compassionate, loving, and wise.

The path of devotion is a path of love and grace, and of seeking union with the divine. It is a path of joy and peace, and of living in harmony with all of life. It is a path of self-transformation, and of discovering the divine within.

CHAPTER VIII

The Wisdom of Silence

The philosophy of silence has been a fundamental part of the Indian spiritual tradition for centuries. It is often said that the highest form of knowledge is found in silence. The wisdom of silence is a way of life that has been passed down from generation to generation, and it is a powerful tool for inner growth and transformation.

The ancient Indian sages understood that true wisdom could not be found in words, but rather in the depths of the mind. They believed that in order to unlock the hidden mysteries of life, one must be able to remain silent and still. This is why the practice of silence has been a part of the Indian spiritual tradition for centuries.

Silence has the power to transform a person and open them up to a new level of understanding. It can help to clear the mind and allow the individual to access inner wisdom and knowledge. Silence helps to create a sense of inner peace and clarity, and it can help to open up the mind to new ideas and insights.

The practice of silence is also a form of meditation. It is a way to quiet the mind, free it from the chatter of the outer world, and to allow for inner contemplation and insight. It is a way to connect with the inner self, and to discover the true nature of the soul.

The wisdom of silence is also a way to connect with the divine. It is a way to open up to the truth of the universe, and to experience the beauty and mystery of life. The silence of the mind can help us to open up to a higher level of understanding, and to experience a greater sense of connection with the divine.

The practice of silence can also help to bring a sense of peace and harmony into our daily lives. Through silence, we can learn to let go of our worries and anxieties, and to focus on the present moment. This can help to bring a sense of balance and serenity into our lives, and to allow us to be more in tune with the natural rhythms of life.

The wisdom of silence can also help us to become more mindful of our thoughts and emotions. By being silent, we can observe our thoughts and feelings without judgement, and to gain greater insight into our inner world. This can help us to cultivate a greater sense of self-awareness, and to better understand our needs and desires.

The practice of silence is also a way to cultivate a greater sense of patience and acceptance. By learning to be silent, we can learn to accept life as it is, and to be more understanding and compassionate towards ourselves and others.

The wisdom of silence is an ancient practice that can help to bring about inner transformation and growth. It is a powerful tool for creating a more peaceful and harmonious life, and for connecting with the divine. By embracing silence, we can learn to access our inner wisdom and knowledge, and to create a more meaningful and fulfilling life.

CHAPTER IX

The Nature of Consciousness

What is consciousness? It is a question that has perplexed philosophers and scientists for centuries. The nature of consciousness is a topic that has been studied by many different disciplines, from psychology to neuroscience. It is something that we all experience, yet its exact nature remains elusive.

Consciousness is generally defined as the awareness of self and the environment. It is the ability to think and reason, and to be aware of one's own thoughts, feelings, and experiences. It is also the ability to be aware of the external world. Generally, we are aware of our own thoughts, experiences, and emotions, and we are also aware of the external world around us.

The nature of consciousness has been studied and debated by many great thinkers throughout history. In the ancient Indian tradition, consciousness was seen as a part of the larger field of Brahman, the underlying force of the universe. In this view, consciousness is the fundamental source of all knowledge and experience.

The Vedas, the ancient texts of India, explore the mysteries of consciousness in great detail. They describe consciousness as an infinite and all-pervading force that is both formless and timeless. It is said to be the source of all knowledge, and the foundation of all reality.

In recent years, science has started to explore the nature of consciousness. With the development of neuroscience, researchers have been able to gain a better understanding of the brain and the role that it plays in the experience of consciousness. It has been suggested that consciousness is the result of the interaction between various brain regions, and that it is the result of a complex system of information processing.

In addition to neuroscience, the nature of consciousness has also been explored by other disciplines, such as philosophy and psychology. In recent years, the concept of mindfulness has become increasingly popular, and it has been suggested that mindfulness can help us to become more aware of our own thoughts, feelings, and experiences.

The nature of consciousness is a complex and often mysterious topic. It is something that we all experience, yet its exact nature remains elusive. While science and philosophy have made some progress in understanding consciousness, there is still much that we don't know. In the ancient Indian tradition, consciousness was seen as a part of the larger field of Brahman, the underlying force of the universe. In recent years, science and philosophy have helped us to gain a better understanding of the brain and the role it plays in the experience of consciousness. Whatever its exact nature, consciousness is an essential part of being human, and it is something that should be explored and understood.

CHAPTER X

The Path of Liberation

The concept of liberation has been a core part of Indian philosophical and religious thought for millennia. The path of liberation, also known as Moksha, is the ultimate spiritual goal of Hinduism. It is the attainment of freedom from the cycle of birth and death, and the realization of one's true nature as an eternal being.

The path of liberation is described in the Upanishads and Bhagavad Gita, two of the most important Hindu scriptures. The Upanishads state that the path to liberation is through knowledge and practice of the true nature of reality. The Bhagavad Gita explains the path of liberation as the practice of yoga, meditation, and selfless service to others.

In order to achieve liberation, one must first understand the nature of the self. The Upanishads describe the individual self as an eternal soul, or Atman. This Atman is considered to be one with the universal Self, or Brahman. The individual self is therefore a part of a larger, universal reality.

Once the individual has gained an understanding of the self and its relationship to the universe, the next step is to practice the path of liberation. This includes developing spiritual practices such as yoga, meditation, and selfless service to others. These practices help to purify the mind and body, allowing one to become more deeply in tune with their true nature.

The path of liberation also involves cultivating certain spiritual qualities such as love, compassion, humility, and detachment. These qualities help to free the individual from the cycle of suffering and rebirth. Once one has acquired these qualities, they are able to see the world as one unified reality.

The path of liberation is often described as a journey of self-discovery and transformation. As one progresses on the path, they gradually become more aware of their inner Self and its connection to the universe. They also become more aware of their potential to live each moment in peace and joy.

The path of liberation is not an easy one, but it is a journey worth taking. It is an opportunity to realize one's true potential and to experience the ultimate freedom. By following the path of liberation, one can find true peace and joy in every moment.

2. The Teachings of the Rishis

The Teachings of the Rishis are the ancient wisdom of India that have been passed down for centuries. These teachings include the power of tapas (self-discipline), the mystery of the Vedas, the science of the Upanishads, the path of Vedantic realization, the practice of yoga, the art of meditation, the wisdom of the Bhagavad Gita, the power of mantras, the practice of Ayurveda, and the power of nature worship. All of these teachings offer profound insight into the complexities of life and will help those who seek them to lead a more mindful and balanced life.

CHAPTER XI

The Power of Tapas

Tapas is an ancient practice from India that has been used for centuries to promote spiritual growth and transformation. Tapas is derived from a Sanskrit word meaning "heat" or "to burn", and refers to a process of discipline and self-control. The practice of tapas has been used to cultivate physical strength, mental clarity and emotional resilience.

The power of tapas lies in its ability to help individuals move beyond their comfort zone and develop a greater sense of self-awareness. Tapas is a practice of self-control that can be used to help reduce stress and anxiety, improve concentration and focus, and increase physical and mental strength. By engaging in this practice, individuals can also gain a greater understanding of their own motivations and desires.

Tapas involves making certain commitments to yourself, such as abstaining from certain activities or foods, or engaging in certain activities or meditations. Through these commitments, individuals are able to become more mindful and aware of their actions and reactions. As individuals become more mindful of their thoughts and feelings, they are able to recognize when they are being influenced by something external, and make better decisions that are more in line with their true desires.

Tapas also helps individuals to develop discipline and self-control. Through the practice of tapas, individuals can learn to control their impulses and direct their energy in a more productive way. This can be especially beneficial when trying to overcome addictions, compulsive behaviors, and other unhealthy habits. By engaging in tapas, individuals are able to recognize the triggers that lead to their unhealthy habits and replace them with more beneficial behaviors.

The power of tapas lies in its ability to help individuals cultivate a greater sense of self-awareness and self-control. Tapas helps individuals to recognize when they are being influenced by external forces and to make better decisions that are more in line with their true desires. Through the practice of tapas, individuals can learn to control their impulses and direct their energy in a more productive way. Tapas is an ancient practice from India that can be used to promote spiritual growth and transformation.

CHAPTER XII

The Mystery of the Veda

The Vedas are ancient texts of India that have been revered for centuries as the source of great spiritual knowledge and wisdom. Written in Sanskrit, the Vedas are a collection of hymns, mantras, and ritual instructions that were composed by a variety of sages over several centuries. The four main Vedas are the Rigveda, Yajurveda, Samaveda, and Atharvaveda, and each contains a wealth of knowledge that can be applied to life today. As a result, the Vedas have been studied by scholars and spiritual seekers alike, and their teachings remain relevant to this day.

The mystery of the Vedas lies in the fact that they are incredibly ancient texts and yet they contain a great deal of wisdom that is still applicable in today's world. This is because the Vedas were not just written by one person, but instead were composed by many different sages over hundreds of years. As a result, the Vedas contain a variety of perspectives and ideas that span the course of Indian spiritual history.

The Vedas also contain a great deal of knowledge about the natural world and the laws of nature. This includes a variety of astronomical observations, mathematical formulas, and even descriptions of the human body. This knowledge was likely acquired through the observations of the sages and their interactions with nature.

Finally, the Vedas were also composed as a means of preserving the spiritual knowledge of the sages and passing it down to future generations. As a result, the Vedas contain a great deal of spiritual teachings and guidance that can still be applied to life today. This includes advice on meditation, finding inner peace, and connecting with the divine.

Ultimately, the mystery of the Vedas lies in their ability to remain relevant and applicable to life today, despite being so ancient. This is a testament to the wisdom and insight of the sages who wrote these texts, and it is a reminder of the power of spiritual knowledge and the importance of preserving it for future generations. As a result, the Vedas remain a valuable source of wisdom and guidance for anyone seeking to deepen their spiritual understanding.

CHAPTER XIII

The Science of the Upanishads

The Upanishads are ancient Hindu scriptures that form the core of the Vedic literature. They are the oldest texts of Indian spirituality, containing the essence of Hindu wisdom. They are the foundation of Hinduism, and have been studied and revered by Hindus for thousands of years.

The Upanishads are believed to be the source of many of the philosophical and spiritual teachings of Hinduism. They are often referred to as the Vedanta, or "end of the Vedas." The Upanishads are a collection of short dialogues and hymns, written in Sanskrit and composed by a variety of authors. Most of the Upanishads were written between 1000 and 500 BCE.

The Upanishads are divided into three main categories: the Samhitas, the Aranyakas, and the Upanishads. The Samhitas are the oldest texts and contain the earliest teachings of the Vedic religion. The Aranyakas are a set of rituals and instructions for performing Vedic sacrifices. The Upanishads are philosophical dialogues between teachers and students, which focus primarily on the nature of reality and the spiritual path of liberation.

The Upanishads are considered to be some of the most profound philosophical and spiritual texts of all time. They are a source of wisdom for many Hindus, and are often referred to as "The Science of the Upanishads." The Upanishads contain a wealth of knowledge on a variety of topics, including the nature of the soul, the nature of reality, the purpose of life, and the path to liberation.

The Upanishads are composed of a variety of perspectives. They provide different interpretations of the same fundamental truths. Some of the most important themes found in the Upanishads include the unity of all things, the interconnectedness of all reality, the importance of meditation and contemplation, the power of love and compassion, and the cyclic nature of existence.

The Upanishads provide many practical tools and techniques for living a life of spiritual growth and enlightenment. They emphasize the importance of self-control and discipline, as well as the need to develop an attitude of non-attachment and acceptance. The Upanishads also provide guidance on karma, reincarnation, and the journey towards liberation.

The Upanishads are considered to be one of the most important texts of Hinduism. They have been studied and revered by Hindus for centuries, and they continue to provide a source of wisdom and guidance for many. The Science of the Upanishads is a timeless collection of wisdom and teachings that are essential for anyone seeking spiritual growth and enlightenment.

CHAPTER XIV

The Path of Vedantic Realization

The Path of Vedantic Realization is an ancient system of spiritual practice, developed by the Vedic sages of India. It is a direct path to the ultimate reality of Brahman, the Divine. It is a spiritual path of self-realization and ultimately, liberation from the cycle of birth and death.

The Vedantic path is based on the teachings of the Upanishads, which are part of the Vedas, the oldest scriptures of India. The Upanishads are philosophical texts that discuss the nature of reality, the existence of Brahman, and the relationship between the individual soul (atman) and the Divine.

The Vedantic path begins with the study of the scriptures and the teachings of the Vedas. Once these are mastered, the practitioner moves onto the practice of meditation and introspection. Through meditation, the practitioner is able to gain deeper insight into the nature of reality and the Divine. Through introspection, the practitioner is able to gain a better understanding of the self and its relationship with the Divine.

The Vedantic path then leads to the practice of yoga. Yoga is an ancient system of physical, mental, and spiritual exercises, designed to bring the practitioner closer to the Divine. Through yoga, the practitioner is able to gain greater clarity of the self and its relationship with the Divine.

The last step of the Vedantic path is the practice of renunciation. Renunciation is the practice of letting go of attachment to material possessions and desires and instead focusing on the Divine. Through renunciation, the practitioner is able to gain a greater sense of peace and freedom from the cycle of birth and death.

The Path of Vedantic Realization is not an easy one. It requires dedication and commitment, as well as courage to face one's own inner truths. However, those who follow this path are rewarded with the ultimate realization of Brahman and the peace and freedom that comes with it. The wisdom of the Vedas, the teachings of the Upanishads, and the practice of yoga and renunciation all serve to bring the practitioner closer to the ultimate truth, the Divine.

CHAPTER XV

The Practice of Yoga

The practice of yoga has been around for thousands of years, and it has been a part of the culture of India since ancient times. In the ancient Vedic texts of India, we find references to yoga being practiced by the seers and sages who sought to understand the mysteries of the universe. The practice of yoga has evolved over the centuries and is still practiced today by millions of people around the world.

Yoga is a practice which helps to bring about physical and mental balance. It is an ancient practice that includes physical postures, breath control and meditation. The practice of yoga can help to reduce stress, increase flexibility, and improve concentration and overall health.

Yoga is based on the belief that the body and mind are connected and can be harmonized through the practice of asanas (postures) and pranayama (breathing exercises). The physical postures are designed to strengthen, stretch and relax the body while improving circulation and digestion. The breathing exercises help to calm the mind and reduce stress. The practice of yoga also helps to increase self-awareness and focus on the present moment.

The practice of yoga is not limited to physical postures and breathing exercises. It also includes meditation which helps to create a sense of peace and harmony. Meditation helps to bring clarity to the mind and connect with the divine.

Yoga has been used for thousands of years as a way of improving health, strengthening the body and calming the mind. In India, it has been an integral part of spiritual practice and as a way of life. Today, yoga is practiced all over the world, and is becoming increasingly popular.

The practice of yoga is not just about physical postures, but also about connecting with the divine. It is about finding inner peace and connecting with the universe. It is about finding balance and harmony between the body, mind and spirit. It is a practice that can be used to achieve physical, mental and spiritual well-being.

The practice of yoga can help to bring about a sense of peace and balance in the body and mind. It can help to reduce stress and improve overall health. It can help to improve flexibility, strength and concentration. And it can help to bring about a deeper understanding of the self and a connection with the divine.

The practice of yoga is a journey of self-discovery and a way to connect with the divine. It is a practice that can help to bring about physical, mental and spiritual well-being. It is a practice that has been around for thousands of years and is still practiced today by millions of people around the world.

CHAPTER XVI

The Art of Meditation

Meditation is an ancient practice that has been used by people of many cultures and religions for thousands of years. It is a way to connect with the inner self and to achieve higher states of consciousness. In India, meditation is an important part of the spiritual tradition and has been practiced since ancient times. The wisdom of lost Bharat, or ancient India, has much to offer in terms of the art of meditation.

To begin, one must understand the purpose of meditation. It is a way to quiet the mind and to connect with the deepest part of oneself. It is a way to find peace, clarity and understanding. It is not meant to be a form of escape, but rather a way to explore the inner realm and gain insights into the greater truth.

When practicing the art of meditation, it is important to have a comfortable and quiet space. It is best to find a place where there are no distractions and where one can relax. It is also important to have an open and clear mind. Clear your thoughts and focus on your breathing.

Once the mind is clear, begin by focusing on a single thought or image. This can be anything from a mantra to a symbol. Concentrate on this thought or image, and allow your mind to move freely with it. Do not try to control the thoughts, but simply observe them.

Allow your body to relax, and use your breath to help you stay focused. Once your mind is clear, you can move into deeper states of awareness. Here, you will be able to access higher levels of consciousness and gain insight into the deeper truth of life.

The art of meditation teaches us to be present in the moment. It helps us to find balance and peace in our lives. It can help us to be more mindful of our thoughts and to stay connected to our inner truth.

Meditation is a powerful tool to help us to connect to our inner wisdom. It can help us to gain greater insight into our lives and to find meaning and purpose. As we explore the depths of our inner being, we can uncover the wisdom of lost Bharat and gain access to a higher level of consciousness.

The practice of meditation can help us to create a sense of peace and balance in our lives. It can help us to become more mindful and aware of our thoughts and feelings. It can also help us to heal old wounds and to gain insights into our purpose and destiny.

The art of meditation is a practice that can help us to find inner peace and understanding. By tapping into the wisdom of lost Bharat, we can gain access to a higher level of consciousness and to a deeper understanding of the true nature of our being. Through the practice of meditation, we can awaken our inner wisdom and use it to create a life of balance, peace and joy.

CHAPTER XVII

The Wisdom of the Bhagavad Gita

The Bhagavad Gita, often referred to as the Gita, is an ancient Sanskrit Hindu scripture written over 2500 years ago. It is part of the Mahabharata, an epic poem of ancient India. The Bhagavad Gita is considered one of the most important scriptures in Hinduism, and its wisdom and teachings are revered throughout the world. Its main theme is the battle of life, in which the protagonist, Arjuna, is taught the path of self-realization and enlightenment through the teachings of his divine teacher, Krishna.

The Bhagavad Gita is a spiritual text that offers timeless wisdom for living a meaningful and fulfilling life. It is full of practical advice on how to live in the present moment, how to think and act with integrity, how to cultivate inner peace, how to find balance in life, and how to act with compassion and kindness towards others. It emphasizes the importance of understanding one's true nature and purpose in life, and of following a spiritual path that leads to liberation from suffering and attachment.

The Bhagavad Gita provides a comprehensive view of the spiritual teachings of Hinduism. It outlines the four paths of yoga, which are the paths of action, knowledge, devotion, and meditation. It explains the nature of the soul, the role of karma, and the importance of detachment and surrender to the divine. It also outlines a code of ethics and moral conduct, which is known as the Yoga of Action.

The Bhagavad Gita also provides insight into the concept of karma, which is the idea that our actions have consequences. It explains how our thoughts, words, and deeds create our destiny. The Gita also emphasizes the importance of living a life of service to others, and of developing a sense of detachment from the material world.

The Bhagavad Gita is an incredibly rich source of wisdom and insight. It provides a complete guide to self-realization, enabling us to live our lives with purpose and meaning. Its teachings are timeless and universal, applicable to all cultures and religions. Its wisdom is timeless and ever relevant, providing us with the tools to live a life of balance and harmony. In the words of the Gita itself:

"On this path there is no failure, only success, because even a little effort goes a long way."

CHAPTER XVIII

The Power of Mantras

Mantras are ancient Sanskrit words or phrases that have been used for centuries to invoke spiritual energy and invoke the power of the divine. Mantras are believed to be powerful tools for transformation and healing. They have been used for centuries in Hindu, Buddhist and other spiritual traditions as a way to focus the mind and open the heart to higher states of consciousness.

Mantras are usually associated with chanting and are believed to have the power to purify the mind, body, and soul. It is believed that the sound of the mantra, when repeated over and over, can evoke powerful energies within us and help us to connect with the divine. The power of mantras lies in their vibration, which is believed to be the key to unlocking spiritual growth and transformation.

Mantras are said to be able to remove negative energy and bring positive energy into our lives. They can help us to manifest our desires and attract positive people, situations and experiences into our lives. Mantras can also be used to heal physical, emotional, and spiritual ailments.

The power of mantras is reflected in the ancient wisdom of India. In the Vedic scriptures, mantras are referred to as "words of power" that can help us to access the divine. In the Upanishads, mantras are said to be the language of the gods, capable of bringing peace and harmony to the world.

The power of mantras is also seen in the ancient practice of using them in rituals and ceremonies. Mantras are often chanted during meditation and prayer, and are used as a way to focus the mind and tap into divine energy. They can also be used as a form of protection and to ward off negative energies.

The power of mantras lies in their vibrational energy. When chanted, the sound waves produced by the mantra can have powerful healing effects on the body and the mind. The vibrations produced by the mantra can balance the body's energy system, help to heal physical ailments, and even improve mental clarity and focus.

The power of mantras is also seen in their ability to bring about spiritual awakening and transformation. Repeating a mantra can help to clear the mind and open the heart to higher states of consciousness. It can also help us to access our inner wisdom and connect with our true self.

The power of mantras is evident in the wisdom of lost Bharat. For centuries, mantras have been used in India to invoke spiritual energy, heal physical ailments, attract positive energies, and bring about transformation and spiritual awakening. The power of mantras lies in their vibrational energy, and their ability to open the heart and mind to the divine.

CHAPTER XIX

The Practice of Ayurveda

Ayurveda is an ancient Indian system of holistic medicine that has been practiced for thousands of years. It is based on the belief that health is a state of balance in the body, mind, and spirit, and that good health can be achieved through proper diet, lifestyle, and the use of natural remedies. Ayurveda is based on the principle of dosha, which is a balance of three energy forces in the body: vata, pitta, and kapha. Imbalances in these forces can lead to health issues.

Ayurveda is a comprehensive system of health care that focuses on prevention as well as on treating illness. It is based on the concept of maintaining harmony in the body, mind, and spirit. Through proper diet, lifestyle, and the use of natural remedies, Ayurveda aims to attain and maintain balance in the body, leading to improved health and wellbeing.

The practice of Ayurveda is based on the principle of dosha. According to this principle, each individual has a unique combination of the three doshas: vata, pitta, and kapha. These are the three energy forces in the body and each one is responsible for certain bodily functions. When all three doshas are in balance, the body is healthy and in harmony. When they become imbalanced, however, they can cause physical and mental health issues.

To maintain balance in the doshas, Ayurveda recommends a variety of lifestyle practices, such as proper diet, physical exercise, meditation, and yoga. It also recommends the use of herbs and natural remedies to treat various illnesses. Ayurveda focuses on prevention rather than cure, which is why it is important to maintain a balanced lifestyle in order to stay healthy.

Ayurveda also emphasizes the importance of the mind-body connection. It believes that mental health is just as important as physical health, and that emotions, thoughts, and behavior all affect our physical health. Therefore, Ayurveda recommends using meditation and other relaxation techniques to reduce mental stress and create harmony in the body.

Ayurveda is a holistic system of health care that focuses on promoting balance and harmony in the body. By following its principles, it is possible to maintain good health and wellbeing. Through proper diet, lifestyle, and the use of natural remedies, Ayurveda can provide support to those seeking a healthier, happier life.

CHAPTER XX

The Power of Nature Worship

The power of nature worship in ancient India has been a source of deep spiritual connection for thousands of years. Nature has been a sacred and integral part of the Indian culture since ancient times, and the reverence for nature has been a part of the Indian way of life. The power of nature worship has been seen in many aspects of ancient Indian life, from religious rituals and festivals to the use of natural elements in art and music.

Nature worship has been a part of Hinduism since its earliest days. Hindus believe in the power of the five elements—earth, water, fire, air, and space—and revere them as manifestations of the godhead. Nature is seen as an expression of divine energy and is often worshipped in the form of various deities. Hindus believe that the entire universe is made up of these five elements, and that they must be respected and honored in order to ensure harmony and balance. Nature is seen as a living being, with its own energy and intelligence.

Nature worship has been a part of Indian culture for centuries. The Vedas, the oldest Hindu scriptures, contain several hymns dedicated to nature. These hymns praise the power and beauty of nature, and ask for its protection and sustenance. Nature is also often seen as a mother figure, providing nourishment and sustenance to her children. Nature worship is also seen in the popular festivals and rituals of Hinduism.

Nature worship was also an integral part of ancient Indian art and music. Nature motifs were used in paintings, carvings, and sculptures to represent the power of nature. Natural elements such as leaves, flowers, and animals were often featured in these works of art, and often symbolized fertility, abundance, and protection. Nature was also a common theme in ancient Indian music, with the sounds of birds, animals, and nature often being used in the composition.

Nature worship is still a strong part of modern Hinduism. Nature deities are worshipped in temples, and many Hindu festivals center around nature. Hindus also continue to use natural elements in art and music, and nature remains an important part of the Indian culture.

The power of nature worship in ancient India is a testament to the deep spiritual connection that Hindus have had with the natural world for centuries. Nature has been a source of inspiration and a source of sustenance for Hindus, and its power and beauty continue to be revered to this day. Nature worship in India is an important part of its history and culture, and an integral part of its identity.

3. The Path of Dharma

The Path of Dharma is the ancient spiritual code of India and is based on the principles of righteousness, an ideal of personal qualities, the concept of duty and the practice of self-knowledge. It emphasizes the importance of self-discipline, non-attachment, compassion, service, simplicity and contentment. Following the Path of Dharma helps one to develop a harmonious inner life and brings peace and joy to the world around them.

CHAPTER XXI

The Principles of Righteousness

The Principles of Righteousness is one of the most important concepts in the ancient Indian philosophy of the Wisdom of Lost Bharat. This concept is the foundation of all ethical and moral thinking in Indian culture and is a cornerstone of Indian tradition and culture. The Principles of Righteousness is the foundation of all aspects of Indian life, including spiritual, familial, and social.

The Principles of Righteousness can be divided into five basic principles: Dharma, Artha, Kama, Moksha, and Brahman. Dharma refers to one's moral duties and is the foundation of all ethical and moral behavior. Artha refers to one's material wealth and is the foundation of economic activity. Kama refers to one's desires and is the foundation of enjoyment and pleasure. Moksha refers to one's spiritual liberation and is the foundation of spiritual knowledge. Finally, Brahman refers to one's ultimate truth and is the foundation of all philosophical and spiritual knowledge.

The first of these five principles is Dharma. Dharma is the foundation of all ethical and moral behavior and is based on the concept of Dharma Shastra, which is a collection of ancient scriptures that detail the duties and responsibilities of each person in society. According to the Dharma Shastra, a person should be truthful, honest, and just in their dealings with others. They should also be compassionate, generous, and selfless. A person should also be mindful of their own well-being and the well-being of others.

The second principle is Artha. Artha is the foundation of economic activity and is focused on the acquisition of wealth and material possessions. This principle is based on the concept of Artha Shastra, which is a collection of ancient scriptures that detail the importance of economic activity and the principles of wealth accumulation. Artha Shastra emphasizes the importance of thrift and hard work in achieving financial success.

The third principle is Kama. Kama is the foundation of enjoyment and pleasure and is based on the concept of Kama Shastra, which is a collection of ancient scriptures that detail the principles of love and romance. Kama Shastra emphasizes the importance of fulfilling one's desires in a healthy and responsible manner.

The fourth principle is Moksha. Moksha is the foundation of spiritual knowledge and is based on the concept of Moksha Shastra, which is a collection of ancient scriptures that detail the path of spiritual liberation. Moksha Shastra emphasizes the importance of meditation, prayer, and other spiritual practices in achieving spiritual liberation.

The fifth and final principle is Brahman. Brahman is the ultimate truth and is the foundation of all philosophical and spiritual knowledge. Brahman is based on the concept of Brahman Shastra, which is a collection of ancient scriptures that detail the concept of Brahman and its relationship to other aspects of life. Brahman Shastra emphasizes the importance of understanding Brahman in order to achieve spiritual liberation.

The Principles of Righteousness is an incredibly important concept in the ancient Wisdom of Lost Bharat. These five principles provide a framework for people to live a life of moral and ethical behavior. They also provide guidance on how to properly use wealth and material possessions, how to enjoy life in a healthy and responsible manner, and how to achieve spiritual liberation. By understanding and following these five principles, people can live a life of balance, harmony, and peace.

CHAPTER XXII

The Qualities of the Ideal Person

The ideal person is a person who has a strong moral compass and is able to live according to the highest principles of ethical behavior. This kind of person is not afraid to stand up for what is right and will strive to help others no matter the cost. The ideal person is someone who is honest and trustworthy and always looks for the best in others. They have a strong sense of justice and fairness and always strive to do the right thing.

In ancient India, the ideal person was often seen as embodying many of the qualities found in the ancient Hindu scriptures known as the Upanishads. These qualities included truthfulness, detachment, non-violence, and compassion. The ideal person was one who was deeply rooted in the teachings of Hinduism and was able to embody these teachings in their daily life. This person was also seen as being capable of rising above the material world and living a life of spiritual enlightenment.

The ideal person was also seen as someone who was deeply rooted in the practice of meditation and mindfulness. This person was able to stay in the present moment and be mindful of the world around them. They were able to take a step back and observe their thoughts, feelings, and actions without being attached to them. This kind of person was able to find inner peace and quiet and access the inner wisdom that comes with this kind of practice.

The ideal person was also someone who was deeply rooted in the practice of selfless service. This person was always looking for ways to help others and was willing to put their own needs and desires aside in order to serve others. This kind of person was seen as an example of what it means to be a good human being and was admired for their selfless actions.

The ideal person was also someone who was deeply rooted in the practice of love and compassion. This person was able to see the beauty in all things, including those who may be different from them. They were able to look beyond the superficial differences and embrace the underlying unity that existed between all things. This kind of person was seen as a source of great hope and inspiration to those around them.

The ideal person was also someone who was deeply rooted in the practice of wisdom and knowledge. This person was always looking to learn and grow and was willing to seek out advice and guidance from wise mentors. They were always looking to improve themselves and their understanding of the world around them. This kind of person was seen as a source of great wisdom and guidance to those around them.

The ideal person was seen as someone who embodied all of these qualities and was able to live a life of true virtue and goodness. This kind of person was a source of great inspiration and hope to those around them and was seen as an example of what it means to live a life of integrity and compassion. They were respected and admired for their dedication and commitment to truth, justice, and virtue.

CHAPTER XXIII

The Concept of Duty

The concept of duty is one of the core values that is deeply rooted in the ancient Indian culture, known as the Wisdom of Lost Bharat. It is the foundation upon which all other values and principles are built, and it is the cornerstone of Indian society. Duty is the responsibility and obligation of an individual to act in a certain way for the benefit of society. It is the commitment to fulfill one's role in society, even in the face of difficulty or hardship.

Duty is a concept that is highly valued in India, and it is seen as an integral part of life. In Hinduism, duty is known as Dharma, and it is one of the four core values of Hinduism. Dharma is the moral law or duty that is applicable to all, regardless of their caste, gender, or religion. It is seen as the path of right action, and it is believed to be based on truth and justice. Dharma can be seen as a way to live in harmony with the universe, and to fulfill one's purpose in life.

The concept of duty is also closely related to the Indian concept of Karma. Karma is the concept that every action has an equal and opposite reaction, and that every action has consequences. The belief is that one's actions determine their future, and that one should strive to act in accordance with their Dharma, or duty. This concept of cause and effect is an important part of Hindu philosophy, and it is seen as an essential part of living a good and moral life.

Duty is also closely connected to the concept of Dharma, and it is seen as an important part of the moral code of conduct that is expected from individuals. The concept of Dharma is based on the idea that every individual has a duty to uphold the values of their family, community, and society as a whole. This includes respecting the laws of the land, being honest and ethical in one's actions, and fulfilling one's obligations to others. Duty also involves being responsible for one's actions, being mindful of the impact of one's actions on others, and striving to uphold the values and principles of their community.

In Indian culture, the concept of Dharma is seen as the foundation of all other virtues and values. It is believed that if an individual is able to live in accordance with their Dharma, they will be able to lead a life of harmony and contentment. Duty is seen as a way of living with integrity, and it is essential for the preservation of Indian culture and values. By understanding and upholding their Dharma, individuals are able to lead a life of purpose and meaning, and to make a positive contribution to their society and to the world.

CHAPTER XXIV

The Practice of Self-Knowledge

In India, the ancient practice of self-knowledge has been practiced for thousands of years. According to the Upanishads, the highest truth is to be found within oneself. This is the central theme of the Upanishads and has been passed down through generations, as a way of living.

The practice of self-knowledge is based on the teachings of the Upanishads, which state that the true essence of one's being lies within and can be discovered through self-reflection. Self-knowledge is the process of looking within one's self, to uncover the innermost truths that lie there. Through this process, one can come to understand the true nature of reality, as well as the purpose of life.

The practice of self-knowledge requires a deep and sustained commitment to the process. It is not something that can be done quickly, or in a short period of time. Rather, it requires a lifetime of dedication and practice.

The first step in the practice of self-knowledge is to get in touch with one's true self. This is done by taking time out of your day to simply be with yourself, without any distractions. During this time, it is important to be still and to observe the thoughts and feelings that come up. This is not a time to judge or evaluate these thoughts and feelings, but simply to allow them to pass through without any resistance.

The next step is to practice meditation, as it is an effective tool for deepening one's understanding of the self. Meditation can be done in a variety of ways, such as focusing on the breath or on a mantra. During this time, it is important to be mindful of the thoughts and feelings that arise, and to observe them without judgment.

The third step is to practice self-inquiry. This is the process of asking questions about one's self, in order to uncover deeper truths. This can be done through journaling, talking to a therapist, or simply asking oneself questions. The goal of self-inquiry is to uncover the true nature of one's being, and to gain a deeper understanding of oneself.

The fourth step is to practice self-acceptance. This is the process of accepting and embracing one's true self, regardless of any external judgments or opinions. This is done through learning to love and accept oneself, and to embrace all of one's imperfections and weaknesses.

Finally, the practice of self-knowledge requires a commitment to living in the present moment. This is done by taking time out of each day to simply be in the present moment, without any distractions. This is the time to observe the thoughts and feelings that arise, without judgment or evaluation.

The practice of self-knowledge can be a difficult and challenging process, but it is well worth the effort. Through this practice, one can come to understand the true nature of reality and their place in it. This provides a sense of purpose and connection to the world, and can lead to a life of peace and contentment.

CHAPTER XXV

The Path of Self-Discipline

The path of self-discipline is a concept that has been prevalent in the ancient Indian culture for centuries. It is a journey that requires the individual to take full responsibility for their actions and decisions, and to live with integrity. Self-discipline has been integral to the spiritual and cultural development of the people of India, and it is a cornerstone of the ancient knowledge and wisdom of the Bharat.

The path of self-discipline is based on the idea that the individual has the power to shape their own destiny and make conscious decisions that will lead to a life of fulfillment and abundance. It requires the individual to practice self-control, self-awareness, and self-reflection in order to develop a strong sense of personal responsibility and to make wise decisions. The ancient wisdom of Bharat teaches that when one is able to master self-discipline, they are able to achieve a life of harmony and balance.

Self-discipline is an ongoing process that is comprised of both inner and outer components. On the inner level, it involves developing an awareness of the mind and body and cultivating a sense of inner peace and harmony. This requires one to become mindful of their thoughts, feelings, and actions and to learn how to respond to them in a mindful and constructive way. On the outer level, it involves developing the ability to take action in accordance with one's values and goals. This includes learning to set realistic goals and to take steps towards achieving them.

In addition to the inner and outer components of self-discipline, the path of the wise in Bharat also involves developing a spiritual practice. This includes the practice of meditation and other spiritual disciplines that help to cultivate a deeper and more meaningful connection with the divine. Such practices enable one to become more aware of their innermost thoughts, feelings, and motivations and to develop a greater sense of self-awareness and peace.

The path of self-discipline is essential for those who seek to live a life of wisdom and fulfillment. It requires the individual to take full responsibility for their actions and decisions, to live with integrity, and to develop a strong sense of personal responsibility. By developing a spiritual practice and cultivating a deep connection with the divine, one can become more mindful of their thoughts, feelings, and actions and to make wise decisions that will lead to a life of harmony and balance.

CHAPTER XXVI

The Practice of Non-Attachment

Non-attachment is a concept that is widely found in the ancient wisdom of India, particularly in the Hindu and Buddhist traditions. It is a way of living that is based on the principle of letting go of attachments to material possessions and emotions, and instead focusing on the present moment and the path to spiritual enlightenment. The practice of non-attachment, or aparigraha, is an essential part of the spiritual journey and is a key element of the teachings of Hinduism, Buddhism, and other Indian spiritual traditions.

In Hinduism, the practice of non-attachment is closely linked to the concept of karma, or the law of cause and effect. According to the law of karma, every action has an effect, and these effects can lead to either positive or negative situations. By practicing non-attachment, one is able to break the cycle of karma and free themselves from the cycle of reincarnation. Non-attachment helps one to let go of all material possessions, emotions, and desires that may prevent them from achieving spiritual liberation.

The practice of non-attachment is also seen in Buddhism, where it is known as "the path of detachment." In Buddhism, non-attachment is seen as a way to free oneself from the cycle of suffering, which is caused by attachment to material possessions, emotions, and desires. By practicing non-attachment, one is able to let go of all attachments and instead focus on the spiritual path and the present moment. The practice of non-attachment is also seen in Jainism, where it is known as "non-possessiveness."

In the Bhagavad Gita, one of the most famous Hindu texts, the practice of non-attachment is referred to as the "yoga of detachment." In this text, the practice of non-attachment is described as the path to spiritual liberation and freedom from the cycle of karma and reincarnation. According to the Bhagavad Gita, by practicing non-attachment, one is able to break free from the ego and attachments to material possessions and desires, and instead focus on the path to spiritual liberation.

Non-attachment is also an important part of the teachings of Advaita Vedanta, a branch of Hindu philosophy. In Advaita Vedanta, the practice of non-attachment is seen as a way to transcend the ego and realize the true nature of reality. According to this philosophy, by practicing non-attachment, one is able to experience the unity of all things, and become one with the divine.

The practice of non-attachment is an essential part of the ancient wisdom of India, and has been an important part of Indian spiritual traditions for thousands of years. By practicing non-attachment, one is able to break free from the cycle of karma and reincarnation and instead focus on the path to spiritual liberation. Non-attachment is a key element of the teachings of Hinduism, Buddhism, and other Indian spiritual traditions, and is a powerful tool for transforming one's life and achieving spiritual enlightenment.

CHAPTER XXVII

The Power of Compassion

Compassion is an essential part of life and has been a key virtue in India for centuries. It is a quality that has been deeply embedded in the culture and traditions of the country, known as Bharat. Compassion is a powerful force that helps us to understand the suffering of others, and to respond with kindness, love, and understanding.

Compassion is the root of all virtues and is the foundation of all spiritual growth. It is the quality of responding to the suffering of others with kindness, love, and understanding. Compassion is not only the ability to feel the pain of another, it is the ability to act on that feeling to help alleviate the other person's suffering. It is a powerful force that can help us to overcome our own suffering, and to bring healing and comfort to those around us.

In India, compassion is an integral part of the culture. It is embedded in the ancient wisdom of the Vedas and Upanishads, and is seen as a fundamental part of living a virtuous life. Compassion is seen as a way to connect with the divine, and to show respect for all other creatures. In Hinduism, the practice of ahimsa (non-violence) is seen as an expression of compassion towards all living creatures. The Bhagavad Gita, one of the most important Hindu scriptures, speaks of the importance of compassion, saying "The wise man should treat all creatures as he himself would be treated."

Compassion is also a key part of Buddhism, which has been an important part of Indian culture for centuries. The

Buddha taught that true compassion is an unconditional, non-discriminatory love that is directed towards all living creatures. He said that the only way to achieve true happiness is to be compassionate and kind to all living beings.

Compassion is an important part of Indian culture, and it is widely celebrated in the country. There are several festivals dedicated to compassion and kindness, such as the festival of Raksha Bandhan, which celebrates the bond between brothers and sisters. On this day, sisters tie a sacred thread around their brothers' wrists, symbolizing their bond of love and protection.

The power of compassion is undeniable, and it is a quality that is deeply valued in India. Compassion is the key to understanding the suffering of others and to responding to it with kindness, love, and understanding. It is a powerful force that can help us to overcome our own suffering, and to bring healing and comfort to those around us. Compassion is a virtue that all should strive to cultivate, as it brings peace, joy, and harmony to our lives.

CHAPTER XXVIII

The Practice of Service

Service is an integral part of the ancient Indian ethos, which has been passed down through generations. It is a practice that is rooted in the belief that all of us are connected and that by serving each other we can bring more peace and harmony into our lives. The tradition of service has been around since the days of the Vedas, and has been practiced in various forms throughout India's history.

The concept of service is deeply embedded in the spiritual beliefs of ancient India. Service is seen as a way to purify the mind and soul and to rid oneself of ego and selfishness. It is believed that those who serve others with compassion and selflessness will be rewarded with a balanced, harmonious life. Service is also seen as a way to cultivate humility and to learn from the perspective of others. The practice of service can be found in many of India's ancient scriptures, such as the Upanishads and the Bhagavad Gita.

Service is seen as a way to connect with the divine. It is believed that by serving others, we can tap into a higher power and find deeper meaning in life. Service is also seen as an expression of gratitude, a way to honor the divine by serving others. In the ancient practice of Karma yoga, service is seen as an essential part of the spiritual journey, as it encourages us to become less self-centered and more focused on the needs of others.

Service can take many forms, from offering simple acts of kindness to volunteering at a local charity or helping out in the community. It is important to remember that service can be done in both small and large ways. Simple acts of kindness, such as helping a neighbor with their groceries or offering a smile to a stranger, can have a profound impact on both the giver and the receiver.

The practice of service is also seen as a way of developing self-discipline. By committing to service, we can learn to be more patient, to be less judgmental, and to be more compassionate. The practice of service can also help us to become more mindful of our actions and to cultivate a greater sense of gratitude for all that we have.

The wisdom of service taught in ancient India is still relevant today. By connecting with the divine through service, we can learn to be more selfless, compassionate, and mindful of our actions. We can also learn to be more grateful, humble, and open-minded. The practice of service can help us to live a more meaningful and fulfilling life, and to bring more peace and harmony into the world.

CHAPTER XXIX

The Virtues of Simplicity

The virtue of simplicity is one of the most important aspects of the ancient Indian philosophy known as the Wisdom of Lost Bharat. This philosophy emphasizes the importance of living a simple life and avoiding unnecessary complexities. In the words of the ancient Indian sage, Mahatma Gandhi, "There is more to life than increasing its speed." The virtue of simplicity teaches us to slow down and enjoy the moments of life as they come.

In the Wisdom of Lost Bharat, simplicity is seen as an antidote to the materialistic and consumerist lifestyle that has become commonplace in modern times. Simplicity involves living without the need for material possessions or accumulation of wealth. It encourages us to focus on developing our inner resources and relationships with others, rather than on material possessions. Simplicity also involves living in harmony with nature and the environment, and cultivating a sense of gratitude for all that we have.

Simplicity is a key element of the Wisdom of Lost Bharat, as it helps us to lead a meaningful and fulfilling life. By living simply, we can focus on developing our inner strength and resilience, and become better able to cope with life's challenges. It also teaches us to live with gratitude and contentment, rather than striving for material gain. Through living simply, we can also make better use of our time and resources, which leads to greater productivity and effectiveness.

The virtue of simplicity helps us to lead a more meaningful life by encouraging us to focus on what really matters. By simplifying our lives, we can make time to spend with our families, friends, and in nature. We can also devote more time to our hobbies and interests, and take up activities that bring us joy and pleasure. Simplicity also allows us to better connect with our spiritual selves, as it encourages us to practice meditation and mindfulness.

Finally, the virtue of simplicity can help us to live a more sustainable lifestyle. By reducing our consumption and waste, we can help to preserve the environment and the planet. We can also make more conscious choices about the products we buy, and support ethical and sustainable businesses.

In conclusion, the virtue of simplicity is an important aspect of the ancient Indian philosophy known as the Wisdom of Lost Bharat. This philosophy encourages us to lead a simpler and more meaningful life, by avoiding material possessions and focusing on developing our inner resources. By living simply, we can make better use of our time and resources, and devote more time to our families, friends, and hobbies. Furthermore, simplicity can help us to live a more sustainable lifestyle, and make better choices about the products we buy.

CHAPTER XXX

The Practice of Contentment

Contentment is a practice that has been respected and valued in the ancient Indian culture. According to the ancient Indian philosophy, contentment is a state of satisfaction and inner peace. It is the ability to accept whatever life offers without desires or attachments.

The practice of contentment is found in many of the ancient Indian texts such as the Upanishads, the Bhagavad Gita, and the Mahabharata. In these texts, contentment is seen as a state of equilibrium where one is able to accept the situation as it is and is free from the attachments to desires and outcomes. This practice is often seen as the ultimate goal of life.

The practice of contentment is a way of life in the ancient Indian culture. It is seen as a way to cultivate inner peace, balance, and joy. It is a practice of self-awareness, of being mindful of the present moment and accepting whatever comes our way. It is a practice of not being attached to outcomes, of not clinging to desires and instead accepting the present moment as it is.

In the ancient Indian culture, contentment was seen as a way of life. It was seen as a way to cultivate inner peace and balance. It was seen as a way to let go of attachments and desires, and instead, accept the present moment as it is.

In the Bhagavad Gita, Krishna tells Arjuna to be content with whatever comes his way. He encourages Arjuna to practice contentment rather than trying to get what he wants. This is the same message in the Upanishads, which suggest that contentment is an important practice to cultivate inner peace and joy.

The practice of contentment is also found in the Mahabharata. Here, Yudhishthira is seen as an example of contentment. He is able to accept whatever comes his way without attachment or desire. He accepts his circumstances as they are and learns to be content with what he has.

The practice of contentment is an important part of the ancient Indian culture. It is a way to cultivate inner peace and joy, and to accept whatever comes our way without clinging to desires or attachments. It is a practice of self-awareness, of being mindful of the present moment, and of accepting the present moment as it is. This is how the ancient Indian culture valued the practice of contentment.

4. The Science of the Mind

The Science of the Mind is the study of the mental processes and their influence on the physical body and behavior. It includes understanding the power of attention, the practice of concentration, the art of self-awareness, the science of breathing, the power of visualization, the practice of positive thinking, the wisdom of self-control, the power of right speech, and the art of listening. By studying the Science of the Mind, we can learn to better understand and control our thoughts, emotions, and behaviors, leading to greater health and well-being.

CHAPTER XXXI

The Nature of the Mind

The concept of the mind has been an integral part of Indian philosophy and has been discussed in the Upanishads, the Bhagavad Gita, and other texts. The Vedic view of the mind is an interesting one. It is believed that the mind is the storehouse of all knowledge, and that it can be used to understand the nature of reality. It is also believed that the mind is composed of three components: the conscious mind, the unconscious mind, and the higher mind.

The conscious mind is the part of the mind that is aware of the present moment. It is the part of the mind that is used to think, reason, and make decisions. The conscious mind is the part of the mind that is in control and is responsible for the decisions we make.

The unconscious mind is the part of the mind that is not conscious and is not in control. It is the part of the mind that stores memories, beliefs, and experiences. The unconscious mind can be seen as the storehouse of all information and knowledge, but it is not always accessible to the conscious mind.

The higher mind is the part of the mind that is responsible for spiritual growth and insight. It is the part of the mind that is responsible for understanding the deeper meaning of life and the nature of reality. It is the part of the mind that helps us to understand what is truly important in life.

The Vedic view of the mind is very different from the Western view of the mind. In the West, the mind is seen as a machine that is operated by the conscious mind. In the Vedic view, the mind is seen as a dynamic system that contains both conscious and unconscious elements. It is believed that the mind is capable of both physical and spiritual growth.

The Vedic view of the mind is an interesting one. It is believed that the mind is capable of great insight and understanding, and that it can be used to understand the nature of reality. It is believed that the mind can be used to access knowledge and insight, and that it can be used to gain wisdom and understanding. The Vedic view of the mind is an important part of the Wisdom of Lost Bharat, and it is important to understand its implications.

CHAPTER XXXII

The Power of Attention

Attention is a powerful tool that can be used to unlock our inner wisdom. In the ancient Indian tradition, attention is seen as a form of meditation, a way to tap into the divine energy that exists within every person. This energy can be used to gain insight into the true nature of reality, to gain clarity of thought, and to access the power of creativity.

The power of attention can be used to bring about transformation in our lives. By focusing our attention on the present moment, we can tap into the spiritual potential within us. By redirecting our attention from the distractions of life and focusing on our inner world, we can open ourselves up to a new level of awareness and understanding.

The power of attention can also be used to help us break free from our own limiting beliefs and patterns. By focusing on the present moment, we can observe our thoughts and feelings without getting caught up in them. This allows us to step back and gain a new perspective on our lives.

The power of attention can also be used to cultivate a sense of inner peace and balance. By focusing on the present moment, we can become aware of the deep connection we have with the universe. We can use this awareness to open ourselves up to the power of love and compassion and to cultivate a sense of contentment and joy.

Attention is also an important tool for developing our intuition. By taking some time each day to focus on our inner being, we can open up to the wisdom of our intuition.

This can help us make better decisions and find creative solutions to our problems.

The power of attention can also be used to cultivate a greater appreciation for life. By focusing on the present moment, we take time to appreciate the beauty and joy of life. We can open ourselves up to the wonders of the world around us and to the joy of connecting with others.

The power of attention is a powerful tool that can help us access our inner wisdom. By redirecting our attention from the distractions of life and focusing on the present moment, we can open ourselves up to a new level of awareness and understanding. This can help us break free from our own limiting beliefs and patterns, cultivate a sense of inner peace and balance, develop our intuition, and cultivate a greater appreciation for life.

CHAPTER XXXIII

The Practice of Concentration

Concentration is the ability to focus and direct one's attention and mental faculties. It has been a central practice in ancient India for centuries, regarded as essential for spiritual advancement, personal growth, and the attainment of enlightenment. The ancient Hindu scripture, the Bhagavad Gita, even states that 'concentration of the mind is the way to perfection.'

The practice of concentration was developed by ancient Indian sages and is found in various spiritual traditions such as yoga, tantra and Buddhism. It has been an important part of the Vedic and yogic teachings since the earliest times. The ancient sages taught that concentration was the key to unlocking the higher realms of spiritual insight and wisdom.

The practice of concentration was seen as a way to develop a deep connection with the divine and to cultivate a powerful inner strength. Ancient Indian texts on concentration, such as the Yoga Sutras of Patanjali, describe the practice as a way of unifying the mind and developing a single-pointed focus. This type of focused attention was seen as the key to unlocking the higher realms of consciousness and understanding.

The ancient sages taught that the practice of concentration requires complete dedication and effort. It involves focusing on a single object or thought for a period of time without any external distractions. This type of practice was seen as a way of quieting the mind and allowing the practitioner to go beyond the ordinary limits of the physical world.

In addition to the practice of concentration, ancient Indian sages also taught the importance of meditation. Meditation was seen as a way of connecting to the divine and transcending the physical realm. It was believed that meditation could lead to a deeper understanding of the self and the world around us.

The practice of concentration was seen as essential for spiritual progress because it helped the practitioner to cultivate a powerful inner strength and a deep connection with the divine. Ancient Indian texts describe concentration as a way of unifying the mind and developing a single-pointed focus. The practice of concentration was also used as a way of developing a strong sense of mental clarity, increasing awareness and insight, and deepening understanding.

The practice of concentration was seen as essential for spiritual advancement in ancient India. It is still used today as a way to cultivate inner strength and to deepen one's connection with the divine. The practice of concentration can help us to quiet our minds, become more aware of the world around us, and to cultivate a powerful inner strength.

CHAPTER XXXIV

The Art of Self-Awareness

The Art of Self-Awareness is an ancient practice rooted in the wisdom of lost Bharat. It is a form of mindful living that allows us to understand our true nature, create meaningful connections with others, and cultivate joy and peace within ourselves.

Self-awareness is the foundation of any meaningful relationship and is essential in order to achieve true fulfilment in life. It is the capacity to observe and understand your own thoughts, feelings and actions. Through self-awareness, we can gain insight into our behavior, motivations, emotions, and beliefs. This understanding can help us to make better decisions, cultivate healthier relationships, and create a more fulfilling life.

Self-awareness is not just about understanding ourselves, it is also about understanding how we interact with the world around us. Our thoughts and feelings affect our behavior and interactions with other people. Through self-awareness, we can become more aware of our own beliefs and biases, as well as how our actions can affect others. We can learn to take responsibility for our behavior and to treat others with respect and kindness.

Self-awareness is not something that can be achieved overnight, it is an ongoing process that requires regular practice and reflection. There are many different techniques that can be used to cultivate self-awareness, such as meditation, journaling, and mindful movement.

One of the most important aspects of self-awareness is being mindful of our thoughts and feelings. Mindfulness can help us to be more aware of our current experience, to observe our thoughts and feelings without judging or reacting to them. This can help us to become more aware of our reactions to difficult situations, and to understand why we may be feeling a certain way.

Self-awareness also involves understanding our own values, goals, and beliefs. This can help us to make decisions that are in line with our values, and to stay true to our goals. We can also use this understanding to create meaningful connections with others, as we will be better able to understand their needs and motivations.

Finally, self-awareness can help us to cultivate joy and peace within ourselves. By being mindful of our thoughts, feelings, and behavior, we can learn to accept and love ourselves for who we are. This can lead to a greater sense of self-acceptance and self-love, which can bring more joy and peace into our lives.

The Art of Self-Awareness is an ancient practice that can help us to understand our true nature, create meaningful connections with others, and cultivate joy and peace within ourselves. Through self-awareness, we can become more mindful of our thoughts, feelings, and actions, and gain insight into our behavior and motivations. This can lead to healthier relationships, better decision-making, and a more fulfilling life.

CHAPTER XXXV

The Science of Breathing

The Science of Breathing is an ancient practice that originated in India, and is now widely used around the world to improve physical, mental and spiritual health. Breathing is the foundation of good health and is essential for life. It is one of the most important aspects of yoga, as it is believed to bring a sense of balance and harmony to the body and mind.

The Science of Breathing is often referred to as Pranayama, which means 'the control of breath'. In this practice, the aim is to gain control over the breath, so that it can be used to bring about a sense of inner peace and balance. Pranayama is an integral part of the ancient Indian practices of yoga, meditation and Ayurveda, and is believed to have many health and wellbeing benefits.

The practice of Pranayama is based on the belief that the breath is an indicator of the state of our physical, mental and spiritual health. In this practice, we learn to use the breath to bring about a balanced state of both the body and mind. By controlling the breath, we can reduce stress and anxiety, and increase our overall wellbeing.

The Science of Breathing is believed to bring about a state of deep relaxation and balance in the body and mind. It is said to help us to connect to our true selves, and to the energy that lies within us. Pranayama can also help to improve concentration and focus, as well as aiding with better sleep.

The practice of Pranayama involves the use of various techniques such as Ujjayi (victorious breath), Nadi

Shodhana (alternate nostril breathing), Bhastrika (bellows breath), Surya Bheda (sun breath) and Kapalbhati (skull shining breath). These techniques are designed to help us gain control over the breath and to regulate the flow of energy throughout the body.

The Science of Breathing is an effective way to improve our overall health and wellbeing. It can help us to reduce stress and anxiety, and to increase our sense of inner peace and balance. Pranayama can be used as a powerful tool to help us to reach a higher level of consciousness and to achieve greater clarity of mind. It is an important part of the Wisdom of Lost Bharat, and can be used by anyone to improve their physical, mental and spiritual health.

CHAPTER XXXVI

The Power of Visualization

Visualization is the practice of using mental imagery to create an image in the mind of something that one wishes to manifest in the physical world. It has been used in many spiritual and healing practices throughout the ages, and its power was known in ancient India, where it was known as darshan. The wisdom of lost Bharat is based on the understanding that the power of visualization can be used to create positive change in one's life and the world around them.

Visualization is a powerful tool that can be used to manifest one's desires and goals. It is an ancient practice that has been used for centuries to create positive changes in people's lives. By visualizing a desired outcome, it is believed that one can bring about a positive change in their life.

The power of visualization is based on the understanding that the mind is a powerful tool, and what we think, we become. If we focus our thoughts on something we desire, it is believed that we can manifest it in the physical world. The key to successful visualization is to create a clear and detailed image of the desired outcome in the mind. This image should be vivid and full of life and emotion, as this will help to bring it into reality.

Visualization can be used to create physical changes in the body, such as healing and relaxation. It can also be used to manifest positive relationships, success, and financial abundance. Visualization can also be used to bring about spiritual growth and enlightenment.

Visualization can also be used to manifest change in the world around us. By visualizing a desired outcome, it is believed that one can bring about positive change in the world, such as peace and harmony.

The wisdom of lost Bharat also teaches that visualization can be used as a form of prayer. By visualizing a desired outcome and then sending that visualization out into the universe, it is believed that one can call upon the power of the Divine to bring about the desired result.

In order to create positive change through visualization, it is important to keep an open mind and heart and to focus on the desired outcome. It is also important to really feel the image in the mind and to stay connected to it during the visualization. It is also important to stay focused and believe that the desired outcome will come to fruition.

Visualization is a powerful tool that can be used to create positive change in one's life and the world around them. The wisdom of lost Bharat teaches us how to use this power to manifest our desires and goals and to bring about positive change in the world. By understanding the power of visualization and applying it in our lives, we can create the life that we desire.

CHAPTER XXXVII

The Practice of Positive Thinking

Positive thinking is an age-old practice that has been embraced by cultures around the world. In India, it is an integral part of the ancient spiritual and philosophical teachings of Bharat. The Wisdom of lost Bharat speaks of the need to cultivate a positive attitude and outlook to achieve success and satisfaction in life.

The basic concept of positive thinking is to focus on the positive aspects of life rather than the negative. This helps to create an environment of optimism and hope, which in turn can help to create a more peaceful and productive life. This practice involves actively looking for and appreciating the good in every situation, seeing the potential in every challenge, and believing in one's self and capabilities. The idea is to stay positive and focus on what can be achieved, rather than focusing on the difficulties and obstacles that may arise.

In the Wisdom of lost Bharat, positive thinking is seen as a form of self-empowerment. It is believed that by shifting one's focus from the negative to the positive, one is able to access the power within to manifest their desired outcomes. This can be done through affirmations, visualization, and mantras. Affirmations are positive statements that are repeated regularly in order to solidify the desired outcome in one's mind. Visualization involves creating a mental picture of what one wishes to achieve and focusing on it until it becomes reality. Mantras are sacred words that are used to create a positive vibration in the mind and body, allowing one to manifest their desires.

The Wisdom of lost Bharat also teaches the importance of cultivating gratitude and joy. By embracing gratitude and joy, one is able to create a sense of peace and contentment, which can help to bring about positive changes in one's life. Gratitude for what one has and joy for what one can become can help to open up new possibilities and opportunities.

In conclusion, positive thinking is an important practice that has been embraced by cultures around the world. In India, it is an integral part of the ancient spiritual and philosophical teachings of Bharat. By focusing on the positive aspects of life, one can access the power within to manifest their desired outcomes. Additionally, gratitude and joy can help to bring about positive changes in one's life. By embracing these practices, one can create a more peaceful and productive life.

CHAPTER XXXVIII

The Wisdom of Self-Control

The wisdom of self-control is an ancient teaching that has been passed down through generations of the people of Bharat, a region in South Asia that is home to many religions, cultures, and traditions. This wisdom has been taught since ancient times, and is still relevant today.

Self-control is the ability to regulate one's emotions, thoughts, and behaviors. It is the ability to maintain composure in difficult situations and make decisions without being swayed by external forces. Self-control is essential for maintaining healthy relationships, making wise decisions, and leading a successful life.

The wisdom of self-control is based on the belief that one must be aware of their own thoughts and feelings before they can control them. The ancient texts of Bharat stress the importance of understanding one's own inner motivation and being aware of the consequences of one's actions. It is believed that by mastering one's own emotions, thoughts, and behaviors, one can make better decisions and lead a more successful life.

One of the most important aspects of self-control is the ability to practice restraint. This means that one should not give in to temptation or act impulsively, but rather take the time to consider the consequences of their actions. This is a difficult skill to master, but it is essential for making wise decisions and avoiding negative outcomes.

Another important aspect of self-control is the ability to remain focused on one's goals. This requires the ability to set priorities and not get distracted by external influences.

It also requires the ability to remain mindful of the present moment and not get caught up in worrying about the future or dwelling on the past. By staying focused on the present and concentrating on one's goals, one can make more informed decisions and achieve greater success.

The wisdom of self-control also teaches that one should practice self-discipline. This means that one should be willing to make sacrifices in order to achieve their goals. It also means that one should not be too hard on themselves when things don't go as planned. One should be able to accept mistakes and learn from them in order to become a better person.

The wisdom of self-control is an important teaching that has been passed down through generations of the people of Bharat. It is a teaching that is still applicable today and is essential for leading a successful and fulfilling life. By mastering one's own emotions, thoughts, and behaviors, one can make better decisions, remain focused on their goals, and practice restraint in difficult situations. With self-control, one can achieve great things and live a life of purpose and meaning.

CHAPTER XXXIX

The Power of Right Speech

The power of right speech is one of the most important concepts in Indian thought. It is seen as a key to unlocking one's full potential, both spiritually and physically. In ancient texts, right speech is closely linked to morality and truthfulness, and is seen as a way to develop a harmonious relationship with the world. This article will explore the concept of right speech in Indian thought, discussing its importance and how it can be applied to modern life.

The concept of right speech is seen in many ancient texts, including the Vedas, Upanishads, and Bhagavad Gita. In the Vedas, the power of right speech is seen as a way to bring harmony and balance to one's life. The text states that "true speech is the mirror of the soul," and that "verily, right speech is the highest of all virtues." Similarly, the Upanishads refer to right speech as a way to attain spiritual awakening. The text states that "speech that is true and without guile" is the path to enlightenment.

The Bhagavad Gita, one of the most important Hindu texts, also celebrates the power of right speech. It states that "true speech is the source of all good deeds" and "the path to truth and freedom." It also states that "the one who speaks truthfully and without guile will be blessed with divine prosperity." These passages emphasize the importance of using truthful and honest speech in order to achieve harmony and balance.

In Indian thought, right speech is often linked to morality and truthfulness. The text of the Mahabharata states that "if one speaks the truth, one attracts the favor of the gods." Similarly, the Mahabharata states that "truthful speech is the highest law." These passages emphasize the importance of speaking the truth and avoiding falsehood in order to live a moral and truthful life.

In modern life, the power of right speech can be applied in a variety of contexts. For example, it can be used to create positive relationships with others. By speaking kindly and honestly, one can create trust and understanding. It can also be used to spread knowledge and understanding of different cultures and traditions. By speaking truthfully and without prejudice, one can foster meaningful dialogue and mutual understanding.

The power of right speech is an important concept in Indian thought. It is seen as a way to bring harmony and balance to one's life, both spiritually and physically. It is closely linked to morality and truthfulness, and can be applied to modern life in order to create positive relationships and spread knowledge and understanding. While the power of right speech may seem simple, it has the potential to be a powerful tool that can bring great benefit to individuals and society as a whole.

CHAPTER XL

The Art of Listening

The Art of Listening is one of the most important aspects of the Wisdom of Lost Bharat. Bharat was a civilization that flourished for thousands of years and produced some of the world's most influential thinkers and leaders. Indeed, the Wisdom of Lost Bharat is a testament to the importance of listening and understanding one another.

The art of listening is an essential part of the Wisdom of Lost Bharat. Bharat was a culture which valued the ability to listen deeply, to understand what was being said, and to respond accordingly. Listening was seen as an opportunity to learn, to gain insight, and to build relationships. Listening was seen as a form of respect, and as a way to show humility.

Bharat had a variety of methods which were used to facilitate the art of listening. For instance, the Vedas, a set of ancient scriptures, taught that one should listen to the words of others with an open heart and mind. This means that one should take the time to listen, to consider the other person's point of view, and to respond with kindness and understanding.

In addition, Bharat had a long tradition of storytelling, which was used as a way to share knowledge and wisdom. Storytelling was seen as an important tool for teaching, as it could be used to explain complex ideas and to engage listeners. Bharat also had a tradition of debate and conversation, which were seen as important forums for learning and for exchanging ideas.

The Wisdom of Lost Bharat taught that in order to truly understand one another, one must be willing to listen without judgment. Listening without judgment helps to create an environment where everyone feels safe to share their thoughts and feelings. It also helps to ensure that the listener is truly hearing what the other person is saying, rather than simply assuming what they mean.

In addition, the Wisdom of Lost Bharat taught that in order to be an effective listener, one must be patient and empathetic. Being patient means taking the time to really hear and understand what the other person is saying, rather than rushing to form a response. Empathy means being able to put oneself in the other person's shoes and to consider their perspective.

The Wisdom of Lost Bharat taught that the art of listening was an essential part of communication. Listening was seen as an opportunity to learn, to gain insight, and to build relationships. It was also seen as a form of respect, and as a way to show humility.

The Wisdom of Lost Bharat also taught that in order to be an effective listener, one must be patient, attentive, and open to new ideas. One must be willing to listen without judgment and to consider the other person's perspective. Finally, one must be willing to ask questions in order to ensure that they truly understand what was said.

The art of listening is an important aspect of the Wisdom of Lost Bharat. By taking the time to listen and understand one another, we can bridge the gap between cultures and gain valuable insight into one another's perspectives. By practicing the art of listening, we can create an environment of understanding and respect, and foster stronger relationships.

5. The Path of Knowledge

The Path of Knowledge is an exploration of the powerful and often overlooked process of self-study. It encourages the practice of inquiry, an understanding of the nature of reason, and the principles of logic and argumentation. Along this path, individuals can hone their skills of debate and reflection, and develop the capacity for discernment. Ultimately, this path leads to greater understanding and wisdom.

CHAPTER XLI

The Power of Self-Study

The power of self-study is a concept that has been deeply ingrained in the cultural heritage of Bharat for centuries. It is a belief that one can develop their own knowledge and skills through careful study and practice, regardless of the resources available. This is something that has been passed down from generations of Bharatiya scholars and thinkers, and is still a fundamental part of the way many people approach learning today.

Self-study is a powerful tool for cultivating knowledge and skills. It enables one to explore new ideas and concepts without having to rely on the guidance of an instructor. It also enables an individual to take ownership of their own learning process, rather than relying on someone else to tell them what to do. Self-study can be a great way to fill in gaps in knowledge that may not be available through traditional instruction.

The power of self-study is rooted in the belief that knowledge and skills can be acquired through practice and repetition. This idea is based on the concept that everyone has the potential to learn and develop their skills, regardless of their current level of knowledge. This belief is a cornerstone of Bharatiya culture, and has been a part of the country's educational system for centuries. It is a concept that has been embraced by modern educators, and is now being used in many different educational contexts.

Self-study is a form of independent learning that requires an individual to be self-motivated and self-disciplined. It requires an individual to make a commitment to learning and to put in the necessary effort to achieve the desired outcomes. This can be a difficult task for some, as it requires a great deal of dedication and hard work. However, the rewards of self-study can be great, as it can lead to a greater understanding of a given topic or skill.

Self-study can be used to supplement traditional instruction, or to replace it altogether. It can be used to learn something new, to deepen existing knowledge, or to simply reinforce existing concepts. It is also a great way to develop critical thinking skills, as it requires an individual to analyze and evaluate the material they are studying.

Self-study can be a challenging but rewarding journey. It requires dedication and a willingness to push oneself to learn. However, the rewards of self-study are well worth the effort. It is a powerful tool for cultivating knowledge and skills, and is an integral part of the cultural heritage of Bharat.

CHAPTER XLII

The Practice of Inquiry

The practice of inquiry is an ancient and revered tradition in India that has been used for centuries to help seekers of truth gain a deeper understanding of their own life and the world around them. Indian culture is renowned for its emphasis on the cultivation of wisdom, and inquiry can be seen as one of the primary methods for doing so. Inquiry is the practice of questioning, examining, and exploring one's own mind, beliefs, and experience in order to gain deeper insight and knowledge.

The practice of inquiry can be traced back to the ancient Upanishads, which are some of the oldest and most influential texts in Indian culture. The Upanishads are filled with questions, challenges, and meditations that are meant to awaken the student's inner wisdom and insight. In the Upanishads, inquiry is seen as a tool for gaining clarity and understanding of the true nature of reality. The practice of inquiry is also seen in the teachings of the Buddha, who encouraged his followers to question and explore their own beliefs and ideas in order to gain a better understanding of the world.

In India, inquiry has been used as an important tool for spiritual exploration and self-discovery. The practice of inquiry is seen as an essential part of the spiritual path, as it helps the seeker to develop a deeper understanding of the nature of reality and one's place in it. In the Hindu tradition, inquiry is seen as a way to uncover the truth that lies at the heart of all things. Many Hindu spiritual teachers have used the practice of inquiry to help their students gain insight into their own lives and the world around them.

In India, inquiry is closely linked to the concept of yoga, which is the path to union with the divine. According to yoga philosophy, the practice of inquiry is essential for spiritual growth. Through inquiry, the yogi can gain insight into the true nature of reality and the divine. Inquiry helps the yogi to develop a deeper understanding of their own life and the world around them. Inquiry can also be used as a tool for self-discipline and self-awareness, as it can help the yogi to identify and address any mental or emotional blocks that may be preventing them from achieving true spiritual awakening.

In the modern world, the practice of inquiry is still used as an important tool for spiritual exploration and self-discovery. Many spiritual teachers and practitioners continue to use inquiry as a way to gain insight into the true nature of reality and the divine. Inquiry can be used to explore the depths of one's own mind and beliefs, helping the seeker to gain a deeper understanding of the world around them. Inquiry can also be used to identify and address any mental or emotional blocks that may be preventing the seeker from achieving true spiritual awakening. Through inquiry, the seeker can gain a deeper understanding of the world and their place in it.

The practice of inquiry is an important part of Indian culture and has been used for centuries to help seekers of truth gain a deeper understanding of their own life and the world around them. Inquiry can be used as a tool for self-discipline, self-awareness, and spiritual exploration. Through inquiry, the seeker can gain insight into the true nature of reality and the divine, helping them to gain a deeper understanding of their own life and the world around them.

CHAPTER XLIII

The Nature of Reason

The Nature of Reason in Ancient India has been a source of debate for centuries. Ancient India was home to one of the oldest civilizations in the world, and its people developed some of the most sophisticated philosophical and spiritual systems. In this article, we will explore the various ways in which the ancient Indians viewed reason and the importance it held in their lives.

The ancient Indians believed in the power of reason and its ability to bring clarity to complex matters. They believed that reason was the only way to understand the world and its workings. The ancient Indians saw reason as the basis of all knowledge, and as such, it was used to make decisions, to debate, and to analyze situations.

The ancient Indians were firm believers in the power of logic and the use of logical reasoning. They used logic to prove their points and to reach conclusions. Logical reasoning was seen as an important tool for understanding the world and making decisions. The ancient Indians valued intellectual debate and the use of logical reasoning in order to understand the world.

Another important concept in ancient India was the idea of Dharma. Dharma was a set of principles that governed the behavior and actions of individuals. It was believed that adhering to Dharma would lead to a better life for all. The ancient Indians believed that reason was a tool that could help people to understand and adhere to Dharma. They believed that reason could help people to make informed decisions and to understand the consequences of those decisions.

The ancient Indians also believed that reason was essential for understanding the spiritual aspects of life. They believed that reason could help one to understand the nature of the soul and the mysteries of the universe. Reason was also used to understand the purpose and meaning of life.

The ancient Indians believed that reason and knowledge were essential tools for living a good life. They believed that knowledge was the key to understanding the world, and that it was essential for making informed decisions. They believed that reason was the key to discovering the truth about the world.

The ancient Indians also believed that reason was the foundation for wisdom. Wisdom was seen as a higher form of knowledge and understanding, and the ancient Indians believed that reason was necessary for attaining it. Reason and wisdom were seen as being closely linked, and it was believed that one could not exist without the other.

In conclusion, the ancient Indians believed that reason was essential for living a good life. They believed that reason was the foundation for knowledge, understanding and wisdom. They saw reason as a tool that could help people to make informed decisions, to understand the world around them, and to understand the spiritual aspects of life. Reason was seen as a key to unlocking the mysteries of the universe and discovering the truth. The Nature of Reason in Ancient India was a source of debate and speculation for centuries, and it is still an important part of the philosophical and spiritual systems of the region today.

CHAPTER XLIV

The Principles of Logic

The ancient Indian civilization has a long and storied history, one that is rich in philosophical and scientific thought. One of the most important aspects of this ancient Indian thought is the principles of logic that were developed in the Vedic period. These principles were based on the Upanishads, the ancient Sanskrit texts, and were the foundation for many of the philosophical debates and discussions that would take place in the centuries to come.

The ancient Indian philosophers believed that the universe is composed of three essential aspects—prakriti (nature), purusha (soul), and atman (self). These three aspects were interconnected and the way they interacted with each other determined the nature of reality. The ancient Indian thinkers believed that the universe was ordered and could be studied rationally. This belief led to the development of logical principles that would help to explain the workings of the universe and the principles of cause and effect.

The principle of identity states that all objects in the universe have a unique identity, which cannot be changed. This principle was important in developing theories about cause and effect and the structure of the universe. The principle of contradiction states that two contradictory statements cannot both be true at the same time. This principle helped to provide clarity in debates and discussions and was used to differentiate between truth and falsehood.

The principle of the excluded middle states that there is no middle ground between two opposites—for example, there can only be one truth or one falsehood. This principle was important in providing a framework for rational thinking and was used to develop theories about the universe and its relationship with the soul.

The principle of non-contradiction states that nothing can be both true and false at the same time. This principle was used to determine the validity of certain statements and to help differentiate between what is true and what is false. The principle of sufficient reason states that every event has a cause and can be explained by rational thought. This principle was used to develop theories about the workings of the universe and to explain cause and effect.

The principles of logic developed in ancient India were an important part of the development of philosophical thought in the region. These principles were used to create discussions and debates about the nature of reality and the structure of the universe. They provided a framework for rational thinking and helped to explain the workings of the universe. The principles of logic in ancient India remain an important part of philosophical thought today, and their impact is still felt in the world of science, mathematics, and philosophy.

CHAPTER XLV

The Logic of Argumentation

The Logic of Argumentation in ancient India has been a source of fascination and scholarly attention for centuries. While much of the philosophical discourse of the ancient India was largely based on Vedas and Upanishads, the Indian philosophers also developed a sophisticated system of argumentation and debate, known as Nyaya. This system of logic was developed by the ancient Indian schools of philosophy, and it has been an integral part of the Indian intellectual tradition since ancient times.

Nyaya is one of the six Vedic schools of thought, and its central focus is on the nature of truth and the development of valid arguments. The Nyaya school was founded by the sage Gautama, and its core texts are the Nyaya Sutras. The Nyaya Sutras are divided into four sections, which discuss the nature of truth, the means of acquiring knowledge, the means of refuting false arguments, and the means of constructing valid arguments.

The Nyaya school of thought emphasizes the importance of valid reasoning, and it pays particular attention to the structure of an argument. According to the Nyaya system, an argument must be composed of three essential elements: pratijna (premise), hetu (reason), and upanaya (inference). Each of these elements must be logically consistent, and they must be free from any contradictions. Furthermore, the Nyaya system also emphasizes the importance of establishing a valid syllogism. A syllogism is a type of logical argument composed of two premises and a conclusion. The premises must be true, and the conclusion must be logically derived from the premises.

The Nyaya school also advocates the use of logical fallacies to refute false arguments. A logical fallacy is an error in reasoning, and it can be used to show that an argument is invalid. Nyaya advocates the use of five logical fallacies to refute false arguments. These five fallacies are called pratijna-hetu-anupapatti (the fallacy of false premise), hetu-siddhanta-anupapatti (the fallacy of faulty inference), adhikarana-siddhanta-anupapatti (the fallacy of faulty application), prasanga-siddhanta-anupapatti (the fallacy of faulty conclusion), and samsaya-siddhanta-anupapatti (the fallacy of uncertainty).

The Nyaya system is also closely related to the school of Indian philosophy known as Samkhya. Samkhya is a dualistic school of thought, which focuses on the distinction between the material and the spiritual aspects of reality. The Samkhya school advocates the use of pramana (valid knowledge) to establish truth. This school of thought emphasizes the use of logic to establish truth, and it has also been used to refute false arguments.

The Nyaya system of argumentation and debate has had a significant influence on Indian philosophy and culture. This system of argumentation has been used by Indian scholars for centuries to discuss and debate complex philosophical issues. It has also been used by Indian politicians to argue their positions on various issues. Furthermore, the Nyaya system has been used to develop a variety of legal systems and codes in India.

In conclusion, it is clear that the Logic of Argumentation in ancient India has been an important part of Indian intellectual tradition for centuries. The Nyaya system of argumentation and debate has been used to discuss and debate philosophical issues, and it has also been used to develop legal systems and codes in India. Furthermore, the Nyaya system has been used to refute false arguments and establish valid syllogisms. The Nyaya system is closely related to the Samkhya school of thought, and it has significantly influenced Indian philosophy and culture.

CHAPTER XLVI

The Art of Argumentation

The Art of Argumentation in ancient India has been a subject of great interest among scholars for centuries. The ancient Indian philosophers developed a sophisticated system of argumentation and debate, known as Nyaya, which is still used by Indian philosophers today. This system of argumentation is based on the Nyaya Sutras, which are a collection of four sections discussing the nature of truth, the means of acquiring knowledge, the means of refuting false arguments, and the means of constructing valid arguments.

The Nyaya system of argumentation emphasizes the importance of valid reasoning, and it pays particular attention to the structure of an argument. According to the Nyaya system, an argument must be composed of three essential elements: pratijna (premise), hetu (reason), and upanaya (inference). Each of these elements must be logically consistent, and they must be free from any contradictions. Furthermore, the Nyaya system also emphasizes the importance of establishing a valid syllogism. A syllogism is a type of logical argument composed of two premises and a conclusion. The premises must be true, and the conclusion must be logically derived from the premises.

The Nyaya system also advocates the use of logical fallacies to refute false arguments. A logical fallacy is an error in reasoning, and it can be used to show that an argument is invalid. Nyaya advocates the use of five logical fallacies to refute false arguments. These five fallacies are called pratijna-hetu-anupapatti (the fallacy of false premise), hetu-siddhanta-anupapatti (the fallacy of faulty inference), adhikarana-siddhanta-anupapatti (the fallacy of faulty application), prasanga-siddhanta-anupapatti (the fallacy of faulty conclusion), and samsaya-siddhanta-anupapatti (the fallacy of uncertainty).

The Nyaya system of argumentation has had a significant influence on Indian philosophy and culture. This system of argumentation has been used by Indian scholars for centuries to discuss and debate complex philosophical issues. It has also been used by Indian politicians to argue their positions on various issues. Furthermore, the Nyaya system has been used to develop a variety of legal systems and codes in India.

In conclusion, it is clear that the Art of Argumentation in ancient India has been an important part of Indian intellectual tradition for centuries. The Nyaya system of argumentation and debate has been used to discuss and debate philosophical issues, and it has also been used to develop legal systems and codes in India. Furthermore, the Nyaya system has been used to refute false arguments and establish valid syllogisms. The Nyaya system is closely related to the Samkhya school of thought, and it has significantly influenced Indian philosophy and culture.

CHAPTER XLVII

The Principles of Argumentation

The Principles of Argumentation in ancient India have been a source of great interest among scholars for centuries. The ancient Indian philosophers developed a sophisticated system of argumentation and debate, known as Nyaya, which is still used by Indian philosophers today. This system of argumentation is based on the Nyaya Sutras, which are a collection of four sections discussing the nature of truth, the means of acquiring knowledge, the means of refuting false arguments, and the means of constructing valid arguments.

The Nyaya system of argumentation emphasizes the importance of valid reasoning, and it pays particular attention to the structure of an argument. According to the Nyaya system, an argument must be composed of three essential elements: pratijna (premise), hetu (reason), and upanaya (inference). Each of these elements must be logically consistent, and they must be free from any contradictions. Furthermore, the Nyaya system also emphasizes the importance of establishing a valid syllogism. A syllogism is a type of logical argument composed of two premises and a conclusion. The premises must be true, and the conclusion must be logically derived from the premises.

The Nyaya system also advocates the use of logical fallacies to refute false arguments. A logical fallacy is an error in reasoning, and it can be used to show that an argument is invalid. Nyaya advocates the use of five logical fallacies to refute false arguments. These five fallacies are called pratijna-hetu-anupapatti (the fallacy of false premise), hetu-siddhanta-anupapatti (the fallacy of faulty inference), adhikarana-siddhanta-anupapatti (the fallacy of faulty application), prasanga-siddhanta-anupapatti (the fallacy of faulty conclusion), and samsaya-siddhanta-anupapatti (the fallacy of uncertainty).

The Nyaya system of argumentation also emphasizes the importance of establishing a valid reason for one's argument. This is known as "hetu", and it is used to support the claims made in an argument. Furthermore, the Nyaya system also recognizes the importance of using evidence to support one's claims. The Nyaya system advocates the use of pramana (valid knowledge) to establish truth. This school of thought emphasizes the use of logic to establish truth, and it has also been used to refute false arguments.

In conclusion, the Principles of Argumentation in ancient India have been an important part of the Indian intellectual tradition for centuries. The Nyaya system of argumentation and debate has been used to discuss and debate philosophical issues, and it has also been used to develop legal systems and codes in India. Furthermore, the Nyaya system has been used to refute false arguments and establish valid syllogisms. The Nyaya system is closely related to the Samkhya school of thought, and it has significantly influenced Indian philosophy and culture.

CHAPTER XLVIII

The Power of Debate

The ancient Indians were renowned for their knowledge and wisdom, and the Power of Debate was one of their greatest gifts to the world. Debate was an integral part of life in ancient India, and it was used for both political and intellectual purposes. Debate was a way for people to express their opinions, discuss different perspectives and come to a consensus. It was also a way for people to hone their skills in public speaking and persuasion.

Debate was an integral part of life in ancient India, and it was seen as a way to resolve disputes and disagreements without resorting to violence. This is why debates were held in public forums and in courtrooms. People would present their arguments and then the audience would decide who had the better argument. This allowed for a peaceful resolution of disputes and encouraged people to think critically and logically.

In ancient India, debates were a form of entertainment as well. People would gather to watch debates and enjoy the spectacle. Debates were often held during festivals and fairs, and people would come from all over to witness the spectacle.

The ability to debate was seen as a sign of intelligence and wisdom in ancient India. People who could debate well were admired and respected. Debating was seen as a way to hone one's skills in logic and rhetoric, and it was seen as an important part of education. Many great thinkers and philosophers were known for their debating skills, and they were able to use their skills to influence the decisions of kings and leaders.

The format of debates in ancient India was quite specific. There were two sides to any debate: the affirmative and the negative. The affirmative side presented their arguments first, and then the negative side would respond. The audience would then decide who had the better argument.

In addition to the format of the debate, there were certain rules that had to be followed. For example, the participants had to be respectful of one another and refrain from using insulting language. They also had to avoid using personal attacks or making false statements.

The Power of Debate in ancient India was a major source of knowledge and wisdom. It allowed people to express their opinions, discuss different perspectives and come to a consensus. It was also a way for people to hone their skills in public speaking and persuasion. Debate was an integral part of life in ancient India, and it was seen as a way to resolve disputes and disagreements without resorting to violence. It was a form of entertainment, and it was admired and respected as a sign of intelligence and wisdom. Debating was an important part of education, and it allowed people to think critically and logically. The Power of Debate in ancient India is still seen today, and it is a testament to the wisdom of the ancient Indians.

CHAPTER XLIX

The Practice of Reflection

The practice of reflection, or self-reflection, is one of the most important aspects of ancient Indian wisdom. It is a practice that has been used in India for thousands of years and is still practiced today. Reflection is a process of introspection and self-examination, where one looks at one's thoughts, feelings, and actions in order to better understand oneself and one's place in the world.

In Indian culture, reflection is seen as an essential part of personal growth and spiritual evolution. It is a practice that is used to develop a deeper understanding of oneself and one's relationship with the world. According to ancient Indian texts, such as the Upanishads and the Bhagavad Gita, reflection is seen as a way to discover the answers to life's questions. It is a way to gain clarity and insight, to learn from one's mistakes, and to cultivate wisdom.

The practice of reflection has been part of Indian culture since ancient times. In the Upanishads, for example, reflection is seen as a way to gain knowledge and wisdom. The Upanishads discuss the importance of reflecting on one's thoughts and feelings in order to gain a greater understanding of the world around us. The Bhagavad Gita also talks about the importance of reflection, describing it as a way to gain insight and understanding.

In the practice of reflection, one can take some time to sit quietly and observe one's thoughts and feelings. This can be done in a variety of ways, such as reflecting on a particular event or situation, or simply reflecting on one's life in general. During this time, one can take a step back and observe one's thoughts and feelings from a distance, without judgment or attachment. This can help one to gain clarity, insight, and understanding.

Another important part of the practice of reflection is to take time to reflect on one's actions. This can help one to understand the consequences of their actions and to learn from their mistakes. Reflection can also help one to develop better habits and to become more mindful of their decisions and actions.

In addition to reflection, ancient Indian wisdom also includes other practices that can help one to develop wisdom and understanding. These include meditation, yoga, and spiritual practices. All of these practices can help one to gain insight and to cultivate a deeper understanding of oneself and the world.

In conclusion, the practice of reflection is an important part of ancient Indian wisdom. It is a practice that has been used for thousands of years and is still practiced today. Reflection is a process of introspection and self-examination, where one looks at one's thoughts, feelings, and actions in order to better understand oneself and one's place in the world. It is a way to gain clarity and insight, to learn from one's mistakes, and to cultivate wisdom.

CHAPTER L

The Path of Discernment

The path of discernment, or viveka, is a central concept in ancient India, which refers to the ability to make wise and prudent judgement. This concept is often seen as a central part of the Indian spiritual tradition and is often discussed in the ancient texts. In this article, we will explore the concept of viveka and its importance in ancient India.

Viveka is the ability to differentiate between right and wrong and to make wise decisions. It is essential to have a clear understanding of the consequences of each action before taking any decision. This concept is seen as a key part of the Indian spiritual tradition and is often discussed in the ancient texts.

The Bhagavad Gita is one of the most important ancient texts, which discusses the concept of viveka. In it, Lord Krishna tells Arjuna to use his discernment to make the right decisions. He stresses that it is only through the use of viveka that one can make the right decisions. He also tells Arjuna that without viveka, one cannot make the right choices.

The Upanishads, which are another important ancient texts, also discuss viveka. They tell us that it is only through viveka that one can distinguish between right and wrong and make wise decisions. They also tell us that viveka is essential to achieving spiritual enlightenment.

The Rig Veda is another ancient text that speaks of the importance of viveka. In it, it is said that viveka is the key to understanding the subtle truths of the universe. The Rig Veda also tells us that viveka is essential to making wise decisions and living a meaningful life.

The Mahabharata is another ancient text that speaks of the importance of viveka. In it, it is said that viveka is the key to understanding the truth and making wise decisions. The Mahabharata also states that one cannot make wise decisions without viveka.

The Manusmriti is another ancient text that speaks of the importance of viveka. In it, it is said that viveka is essential to making wise decisions. The Manusmriti also states that without viveka, one cannot make wise decisions.

The path of discernment was an important concept in ancient India. It was seen as a key part of the Indian spiritual tradition and was discussed in the ancient texts. Viveka was seen as essential to making wise decisions and living a meaningful life. It was also seen as essential to achieving spiritual enlightenment. The ancient texts taught us that it is only through the use of viveka that one can make the right decisions.

6. The Science of Society

The Science of Society is the study of the principles, nature, and practices of social organization, power, leadership, governance, dialogue, negotiation, diplomacy, justice, conflict, and reconciliation. It seeks to understand how these elements interact to shape the complex social worlds we inhabit. It looks at the ways in which social forces interact to create and maintain social order, and how those same forces can be used to bring about change and progress. Through an understanding of these elements, it seeks to provide guidance on how to create and sustain healthy, equitable and just societies.

CHAPTER LI

The Principles of Social Organization

The principles of social organization in ancient India go back to the Vedic period, which is believed to have begun around 1500 BCE. In this period, the caste system was established and the four varnas, or social classes, were created. Each varna had its own specific duties and responsibilities, and each one was respected and honored in its own way.

The caste system was based on the principle of division of labor and the division of society into four distinct classes. The four varnas were the Brahmana, the Kshatriya, the Vaishya, and the Shudra. The Brahmana were the priestly class, responsible for conducting religious rituals and performing other religious duties. The Kshatriya were the warrior class, responsible for the protection of the people and the kingdom. The Vaishya were the mercantile class, responsible for the production and distribution of goods. The Shudra were the laboring class, responsible for manual labor and service.

The four varnas were further divided into numerous sub-castes, or jatis, each of which had its own specific occupation and duties. This division of labor was necessary for the efficient functioning of society. People were expected to adhere to their respective caste and not move up or down in social hierarchy. A person's place in the caste system was determined by birth and could not be changed.

The caste system was also based on the principle of purity and pollution. Each caste had its own rules and regulations regarding purity sand pollution and these were strictly enforced. Certain activities were considered polluting and were prohibited. The caste system also regulated marriage, prohibiting marriage between people of different castes.

The caste system was an essential part of ancient Indian social organization. It helped maintain social order and stability by assigning each person to a specific role and responsibilities. It also provided a sense of unity and identity among the people of India by creating a shared system of beliefs and values.

The principles of social organization in ancient India were based on the idea of harmony and balance. The four varnas were seen as four aspects of the same divine being and were believed to exist in perfect harmony with each other. The four varnas were seen as the four legs of a chariot, each of which was necessary for the chariot to move forward. Similarly, all members of society were seen as necessary for the functioning of the society and the maintenance of social order.

The principles of social organization in ancient India were also based on the principle of interdependence. Each caste had its own specific duties and responsibilities and were dependent on each other for the functioning of the society. This fostered a sense of cooperation and mutual respect among the people.

Finally, the principles of social organization in ancient India were based on the idea of justice. The four varnas were seen as equal in their rights and responsibilities, and everyone was expected to abide by the same rules and regulations. This ensured that everyone was treated fairly and with respect.

The principles of social organization in ancient India were essential for the functioning of society. They provided the foundation for a strong, stable, and harmonious society, and ensured that everyone had an equal opportunity to succeed. This system of social organization served as a model for many later societies and helped shape the culture of India for centuries.

CHAPTER LII

The Nature of Power

The ancient Indian civilization was one of the most powerful in the world during its heyday, and its understanding of the nature of power was a significant part of its legacy. Ancient Indians recognized the importance of power, and they often sought to acquire, maintain, and wield it in order to achieve their goals. This essay will explore the various ways in which power was understood in ancient India, and how it was used to influence the culture, politics, and economy of the time.

The concept of power in ancient India was closely tied to the system of hierarchy and social stratification. The various castes and classes in ancient India were given varying levels of authority, with Brahmans (priests) being at the top and the Shudras (laborers) at the bottom. This caste system was largely determined by birth, and it was thought to be divinely ordained. This hierarchical system of power was reflected in the political structure of the day, with the kings and emperors at the top of the pyramid and the common people having little to no say in matters of governance.

The ancient Indians also recognized the importance of religious power. The Vedas, the ancient Hindu scriptures, were seen as a source of divine knowledge and power, and were often used to legitimize the authority of the ruling class. Religion was also used as a means of control, with religious rituals, taboos, and laws being used to maintain order and obedience among the people.

In addition to the power of religion and hierarchy, the ancient Indians also believed in the power of knowledge. The Vedic tradition held that knowledge was the key to unlocking the secrets of the universe, and it was believed that those who had access to knowledge had the power to shape the world around them. This belief was reflected in the culture of the time, with scholars and intellectuals being highly respected and revered.

Finally, the ancient Indians also believed in the power of wealth and material possessions. Wealth was seen as a sign of success and power, and those who had wealth were often seen as being more important than those who did not. This belief was reflected in the economy of the time, with merchants and traders being the most powerful and influential members of society.

In conclusion, the ancient Indians had a complex understanding of the nature of power. They believed in the power of hierarchy, religion, knowledge, and wealth, and they used all of these in order to maintain their authority and influence over the people. Although the systems of power and control in ancient India may have been oppressive and unjust, they were also a reflection of the complex and sophisticated understanding of power that the ancient Indians had.

CHAPTER LIII

The Practice of Leadership

The practice of leadership in ancient India was a complex and intricate system. Leadership was often based on a combination of personal character, virtue, and ability. The practice of leadership was based on the principles of dharma, or righteous conduct.

Leaders in ancient India were expected to adhere to high moral standards in order to be successful. They were expected to be honest, just, and generous. Leaders were also expected to be compassionate, wise, and patient. Leaders had to possess the virtues of humility, courage, and self-control.

Leaders in ancient India were not only expected to behave in a virtuous manner, but to also use their power and influence wisely. Leaders were expected to make decisions that were in the best interests of their people. It was believed that a leader who acted in the best interests of his people would be blessed with success.

Leaders in ancient India had to have knowledge of a variety of subjects in order to make informed decisions. This included knowledge of economics, politics, law, philosophy, and religious matters. It was believed that a leader should be well-versed in all of these areas in order to make wise decisions.

Leadership in ancient India was often passed down through the generations. Leaders were often chosen from the same family or clan. This ensured that the leader was familiar with the needs and concerns of their people. It also ensured that the leader had a deep understanding of the culture, customs, and values of their people.

Leaders in ancient India were expected to lead by example. They were expected to be brave and courageous. Leaders were expected to make decisions that were in the best interests of their people, even if those decisions were unpopular. Leaders were also expected to be generous and charitable.

Leaders in ancient India were expected to lead with kindness and understanding. They were expected to treat their people with respect and to be open to their ideas and opinions. Leaders were expected to be just and fair in their decisions.

Leaders in ancient India were also expected to uphold the principles of dharma. This included being honest, loyal, and honorable. Leaders were expected to be generous and compassionate to their people. Leaders were expected to show respect for their elders and to be humble in their dealings with others.

Leadership in ancient India was a complex and intricate system. Leaders were expected to have a deep understanding of the culture, customs, and values of their people. They were also expected to act in a virtuous and wise manner. The practice of leadership in ancient India was based on the principles of dharma, or righteous conduct. Leaders had to possess the virtues of humility, courage, and self-control in order to be successful. Leaders were expected to lead by example and to make decisions that were in the best interests of their people.

CHAPTER LIV

The Art of Governance

The concept of governance in ancient India is an important element of the study of the culture and traditions of the country. It is believed that the ancient rulers of India followed a set of principles for the effective administration of their kingdom. To understand the principles of governance in ancient India, one must look at the various aspects of the political, social and economic systems of the time.

The political system of ancient India was based on monarchical rule. The king or maharaja was the supreme authority in the government and he was responsible for all the decisions made in the kingdom. The maharaja was advised by a council of ministers, which included officials from the military, the bureaucracy and the religious orders. The maharaja was also assisted by a court of justice, which was responsible for settling disputes and upholding the law.

The social system of ancient India was based on a caste system. This system divided people into different classes based on their social status and occupations. The four major classes in this system were the Brahmins, the Kshatriyas, the Vaishyas and the Shudras. The Brahmins were the highest class in the system and were responsible for spiritual guidance, while the Kshatriyas were the warriors and rulers of the kingdom. The Vaishyas were the merchants and the Shudras were the lowest class, who were responsible for manual labor and service.

The economic system of ancient India was largely based on agriculture. People were largely dependent on the land for their livelihood and the economy was based on the production and distribution of agricultural goods. The maharaja was responsible for ensuring that the farmers had access to the resources they needed to grow their crops. The maharaja also had to ensure that the taxes were collected from the people in order to maintain the kingdom's infrastructure.

The art of governance in ancient India was based on the principles of justice, equity and fairness. The maharaja was expected to be impartial and just in his decisions. He was also expected to provide equal opportunity for all citizens, regardless of their caste or social status. The maharaja was also expected to provide protection to the weaker sections of the society, such as women, children and the elderly.

The art of governance in ancient India also included the practice of dharma. Dharma is a set of principles that guides the moral and ethical behavior of individuals and societies. It is believed that the maharaja had to uphold the principles of dharma in order to ensure justice and order in the kingdom.

The art of governance in ancient India also included the practice of diplomacy and negotiation. The maharaja was expected to maintain good relations with other nations and kingdoms and to use diplomacy to resolve disputes between them. The maharaja was also expected to engage in trade with other countries and to ensure that the kingdom benefited from the exchange of goods and services.

The art of governance in ancient India was an important part of the culture and traditions of the country. It was based on principles of justice, equity and fairness, and it was the responsibility of the maharaja to ensure that these principles were upheld in the kingdom. The maharaja was also expected to use diplomacy and negotiation to resolve disputes with other nations and to maintain good relations with them. The art of governance in ancient India was an important part of the culture and traditions of the country and it continues to be an important part of India's culture and traditions today.

CHAPTER LV

The Power of Dialogue

In ancient India, the power of dialogue was highly valued and respected. The ancient Indian texts, such as the Vedas, Upanishads, Mahabharata, and Ramayana, contain numerous examples of dialogue between gods, goddesses, kings, and common people. Dialogue was often used to resolve conflicts, share wisdom, and make decisions.

The power of dialogue was seen as a way to bring people together, to build relationships, and to create understanding. It was believed that through dialogue, one could gain deeper insight into the true nature of reality. Dialogue was also seen as a tool for self-realization and for developing greater awareness.

The Mahabharata is one of the most well known examples of the power of dialogue in ancient India. In this epic, the Pandava brothers engage in a dialogue with their cousins, the Kauravas, in order to resolve their differences. The Pandavas and Kauravas put forward their respective arguments and eventually reach an agreement. The dialogue in the Mahabharata reveals the importance of understanding different points of view and of finding common ground.

In the Bhagavad Gita, the dialogue between Arjuna and Krishna is another important example of the power of dialogue in ancient India. In this dialogue, Krishna teaches Arjuna the importance of dharma and the power of yoga and meditation. Through dialogue, Arjuna comes to a deeper understanding of himself and his place in the world.

The power of dialogue was also used in the Upanishads. These ancient texts are full of conversations between teachers and their students. Through these conversations, the teachers were able to impart wisdom and knowledge to their students. The Upanishads emphasize the importance of dialogue and the power of questioning and learning.

The Ramayana also contains a powerful example of the power of dialogue in ancient India. In this epic, the dialogue between Rama and Ravana reveals the importance of right conduct and of using one's power responsibly. Through dialogue, Rama is able to bring peace to the kingdom and teach Ravana the importance of dharma.

The power of dialogue in ancient India was also evident in the law books of the time. These books contain a variety of debates, discussions, and dialogues between learned men and rulers. These dialogues often dealt with legal matters, political issues, and the interpretation of scriptures.

The power of dialogue in ancient India reveals the importance of communication and understanding. Dialogue was seen as a way to build relationships, to resolve conflicts, and to gain deeper insight into the nature of reality. Dialogue was used to share wisdom and knowledge, to teach and learn, and to make decisions. Through dialogue, people were able to reach a better understanding of themselves and of their place in the world.

CHAPTER LVI

The Practice of Negotiation

Negotiation was an important part of ancient India's society and culture. It was practiced across all levels of society, from the royal court to rural villages, and was used in a variety of contexts, from politics to trade to everyday life. The practice of negotiation in ancient India was based on the principles of dharma, or the concept of ethical and moral duty. This meant that the parties involved in any negotiation had to be honest and act in good faith, and that all outcomes had to be fair and just.

The practice of negotiation in ancient India was based on the concept of dharmic justice, which emphasized the importance of taking into account the needs of all parties involved. This meant that negotiations had to be conducted in an atmosphere of mutual respect and trust, and that all parties had to come to a mutually beneficial agreement. This was in contrast to the Roman legal system, which was based on the idea of might makes right and could lead to unfair outcomes.

In ancient India, negotiation was seen as a way to resolve disputes and reach agreements between different parties. Negotiations could take many forms, from one-on-one talks to group discussions. In some cases, negotiations were conducted in the presence of a neutral third party, such as a judge or mediator, who could help ensure that the process was fair and just.

Negotiations in ancient India were often conducted using a set of guidelines known as the Sutra shastras. This set of rules and guidelines was designed to ensure that negotiations were conducted in an orderly and fair manner. The Sutra shastras included rules on how to conduct oneself during negotiations, how to present an argument, and how to reach an agreement. They also included rules on the types of evidence that could be used to support an argument.

The practice of negotiation in ancient India was also closely related to the concept of niyoga, or the practice of consulting experts and advisors in order to arrive at a just and equitable outcome. This idea was based on the belief that the wisest decision could be made when different perspectives and experiences were taken into account. The practice of niyoga was often used in negotiations, as it allowed for a more balanced and informed discussion.

The practice of negotiation in ancient India was an important part of society, as it allowed for disputes to be resolved in a peaceful and just manner. It was based on the principles of dharma and niyoga, and was an essential part of the social and cultural life of the time. Negotiation was a way to ensure that all parties involved in a dispute got a fair outcome, and that justice was served.

CHAPTER LVII

The Wisdom of Diplomacy

The wisdom of diplomacy has been an integral part of India's civilization since time immemorial. It is deeply embedded in the Indian culture and forms a core part of the country's political and diplomatic history. The early rulers of India, such as the Mauryas, the Guptas, and other imperial dynasties, displayed a remarkable knowledge and skill in the art of diplomacy. In ancient India, diplomacy was used both as a tool for maintaining peace and order and as a way of achieving political and economic objectives.

The ancient Indian rulers were well aware of the importance of diplomacy. They understood that diplomacy was essential for the stability of their kingdom and the success of their policies. To achieve their objectives, they employed a variety of diplomatic tools and techniques, ranging from negotiations and treaty making to military actions and alliances.

The ancient rulers also had a deep understanding of the importance of maintaining good diplomatic relations with other countries. The Mauryas and the Guptas, for example, maintained good relations with their neighbors. They also engaged in trade and commerce with other countries, which helped to strengthen their diplomatic ties.

The ancient Indian rulers were also skilled in the use of diplomacy to resolve conflicts between states. They realized that the use of force was not always the best option and instead preferred to use diplomacy to resolve disputes. They understood that the use of diplomacy could prevent a war from occurring and could help to bring about a peaceful resolution to a conflict.

The ancient Indian rulers also realized that diplomacy was essential for maintaining internal stability. Diplomatic relations with other countries enabled them to receive valuable information about their enemies and to form alliances that could help protect their kingdom from attack. This allowed them to keep their borders safe and secure, and to protect their citizens from external threats.

Throughout its history, India has used the wisdom of diplomacy to achieve its goals. The ancient Indian rulers understood the importance of diplomacy and used it to their advantage. They understood the importance of maintaining good diplomatic relations with other countries, using diplomacy to resolve conflicts between states, and using diplomacy to maintain internal stability. The wisdom of diplomacy has been an integral part of India's civilization since time immemorial and continues to be a key part of the country's political and diplomatic history.

CHAPTER LVIII

The Principles of Justice

The principles of justice are an integral part of India's rich culture and history. Ancient India had a sophisticated system of justice that was often based on both spiritual and legal concepts. This system of justice was largely based on dharma – the eternal law of righteousness and justice. The principles of justice in ancient India involved a variety of aspects, including the establishment of fairness, the protection of human rights, the prevention of injustice, and the promotion of ethical behavior.

The foundation of justice in ancient India was rooted in the Vedic texts, which provided philosophical, religious, and social guidance. The Vedic scriptures outlined a system of justice that was based on the principles of dharma, or duty. Dharma is the eternal law of righteousness and justice, and it was a fundamental part of the Indian legal system. According to the Vedic texts, a person's dharma is their duty towards the universe and all living beings. This duty included following the laws of justice and living a life of truth, honesty, and compassion.

The Vedic texts also outlined a system of justice that was based on the concept of retribution, or punishment for wrong doing. Many of the texts also set out principles of justice that were based on the concept of karma, or the law of causation. According to the laws of karma, a person's actions have consequences, and these consequences will eventually come back to them. This system of justice was based on the idea that a person should receive punishment for their wrongdoings and be rewarded for their good deeds.

The ancient Indian system of justice was also based on the concept of justice as fairness, or the idea that all people should be treated equally under the law. This principle of justice was often seen in the form of the caste system in ancient India. The caste system was a hierarchical social structure in which people were divided into different castes based on their birth, and each caste had certain rights and responsibilities. This system of justice was based on the idea that everyone should have access to the same rights and opportunities regardless of their birth.

The laws of justice in ancient India also included the concept of religious freedom. The Vedic texts outlined a system of justice that respected the freedom of religious belief, and the right to practice religious beliefs without interference or discrimination. This principle of justice was important to the ancient Indians, as they believed that all people should be free to practice their own religious beliefs and should not be forced to convert to another religion.

The laws of justice in ancient India also included the concept of equality before the law. This principle of justice was based on the idea that everyone should have equal access to justice and equal protection under the law. This principle of justice was important to the ancient Indians, as they believed that no one should be placed above the law.

The principles of justice in ancient India were not always perfect, and there were certainly instances of injustice and inequality in the society. However, the overall system of justice in ancient India was based on the principles of dharma, karma, justice as fairness, religious freedom, and equality before the law. These principles of justice laid the foundation for the development of a strong and just legal system in India today.

CHAPTER LIX

The Nature of Conflict

Conflict has been an inherent part of human society since time immemorial, and India is no exception. The nature of conflict in ancient India varied in its form, intensity and causes, but it nonetheless had a major impact on the development of the region. In this essay, we will explore the various types of conflict that were present in ancient India, as well as their causes, effects and how they were dealt with.

One of the most common forms of conflict in ancient India was the struggle for power. This could take the form of inter-kingdom wars, civil wars, or even conflict between powerful individuals or families. This struggle for power was often motivated by a desire to expand one's kingdom or to gain control of resources. This kind of conflict was not uncommon throughout history, and it was present in ancient India as well.

Another form of conflict in ancient India was social strife, which was caused by disparities in wealth, power and status. This kind of conflict could take the form of caste conflicts, religious conflicts, or conflicts between different social classes. These conflicts could have devastating effects on the society, leading to violence, poverty and other social problems.

Conflict was also present in the form of economic struggles. This could take the form of trade wars between rival kingdoms, or even disputes over resources such as land and water. Economic struggles often led to conflict between different social classes, and it was a major factor in the rise of powerful empires in ancient India.

The nature of conflict in ancient India was also shaped by the religious beliefs of the people. Conflicts between religious groups were common, and these conflicts could be violent and destructive. Religious conflicts were often used as a tool to gain power or resources, and they could have far-reaching effects on the society.

Finally, conflicts between foreign powers were also present in ancient India. These conflicts were often driven by a desire to gain control of resources or to expand their respective empires. These conflicts were often intense and destructive, and they could have a major impact on the development of the region.

Overall, the nature of conflict in ancient India varied in its form, intensity and causes, but it nonetheless had a major impact on the development of the region. This essay has explored the various types of conflict that were present in ancient India, as well as their causes, effects and how they were dealt with. It is clear that conflict was an integral part of the history of India, and it had a profound effect on the development of the region.

CHAPTER LX

The Power of Reconciliation

Reconciliation is an ancient and powerful concept that has been present in India since ancient times. It is a practice of building relationships between two or more parties in order to resolve conflict and promote peace. Reconciliation is a process that can involve forgiveness, compromise and understanding. The power of reconciliation can be seen in the ancient scriptures of India, which emphasize the importance of understanding and finding common ground between people.

In the Hindu scriptures, the Bhagavad Gita, Krishna teaches the importance of reconciliation. He says, "The wise do not quarrel with one another; for the foolish quarrel with one another and perish." Krishna is encouraging his disciples to seek harmony and understanding instead of fighting and arguing. This is an important lesson for all of us today.

The Vedic scriptures also speak to the power of reconciliation. The Upanishads say, "The highest of all reconciliations is to understand and appreciate all differences." This means that we should strive to understand the perspectives of those who are different from us. When we are able to do this, we are able to find common ground and work towards resolving our differences without resorting to conflict.

The ancient science of yoga also speaks to the power of reconciliation. Yoga is a practice of stilling the mind and connecting to the inner wisdom that lies within us. When we practice yoga, we are able to cultivate a sense of peace and understanding. This helps us to see the perspectives of others without judgement and to find common ground.

The ancient Indian wisdom of reconciliation also speaks to the power of truth. The Vedas say, "Truth is the highest of all reconciliations." This means that we should seek to understand the truth in any given situation and strive to find a resolution that is based on truth. This is an important concept that can help us to resolve any conflicts that arise.

The ancient Indian wisdom of reconciliation also speaks to the power of compassion. The Upanishads say, "The highest of all reconciliations is compassion." This means that we should strive to understand the perspectives of those around us and seek to resolve our differences with compassion and understanding.

The ancient Indian wisdom of reconciliation has much to teach us today. It reminds us that conflict is not always necessary and that understanding and finding common ground is the most powerful way to resolve disputes. Reconciliation is a powerful tool that can help us to build relationships and create peace. It is an ancient and powerful concept that has been present in India since ancient times and continues to be relevant today.

7. The Art of Life

The Art of Life is a philosophy that encourages its adherents to embrace the creative power within themselves, to express themselves fully and authentically, to find beauty in all aspects of life, to adhere to aesthetic principles, to live in harmony with others, to cultivate strong and meaningful friendships, to practice compassion, to appreciate joy, to experience the power of love, and to express gratitude. It is an inspiring and meaningful way to live life.

CHAPTER LXI

The Power of Creativity

Creativity is an essential part of life and has been part of the Indian culture since ancient times. In ancient India, creativity was seen as a source of power and was highly valued. Creative people were looked up to and respected, and their works were seen as a reflection of divine power.

The power of creativity was seen in the ancient Vedic literature, where creativity was seen as a form of godly energy. The Rig Veda, for example, speaks of the creative power of gods and goddesses. It describes how they created the world out of nothing and how they used their creative power to bring life to it.

The Vedas also describe how creativity was used in different aspects of life. It was used in the construction of homes and temples, in the making of tools and weapons, and in the creation of art and music. Creativity was also used in the creation of literature, poetry, and philosophy.

The power of creativity was seen in the works of great poets and writers, who used their imagination to create stories and poems. The Mahabharata is one of the greatest works of literature from ancient India, and it was written by the great poet Vyasa.

The art of ancient India was also highly creative. The cave paintings of Ajanta and Ellora are examples of the creative power of the artists. The sculptures of Khajuraho and the temples of the Chola kingdom are other examples of the creative power of the people of ancient India.

The power of creativity was also seen in the development of science and technology in ancient India.

The Vedas contain instructions for creating various tools and instruments, and the ancient Indians used their creativity to develop these tools and instruments.

The power of creativity was also used in the development of philosophy and religion in ancient India. The Upanishads contain some of the most profound philosophical thoughts of the ancient Indians, and these thoughts were developed through the use of creative thought.

The power of creativity was also seen in the development of the great epics of ancient India. The Ramayana and the Mahabharata are some of the greatest works of literature in the world, and they were written through the use of creative thought.

The power of creativity was also seen in the development of medicine in ancient India. Ayurveda, the traditional system of medicine, was developed through the use of creative thought.

The power of creativity was also seen in the development of the great cities of ancient India. The cities of Harappa and Mohenjo-Daro were developed through the use of creative thought and planning.

The power of creativity was also seen in the development of mathematics and astronomy in ancient India. The Vedangas, the ancient texts on mathematics, were developed through the use of creative thought.

The power of creativity was also seen in the development of music in ancient India. The Sangeet Natak, a collection of musical compositions, was developed through the use of creative thought.

The power of creativity was also seen in the development of art and architecture in ancient India. The great palaces and forts of ancient India were developed through the use of creative thought.

The power of creativity was highly valued in ancient India, and it was seen as an essential part of life. Creative people were respected and their works were seen as a reflection of divine power. The great works of literature, art, philosophy, and science of ancient India were all developed through the use of creative thought. The power of creativity has been an essential part of Indian culture since ancient times, and it continues to be an important part of life today.

CHAPTER LXII

The Practice of Self-Expression

The practice of self-expression was an important part of life in ancient India. It was believed that through the art of self-expression, one could gain insight into their true nature and develop a deeper understanding of the universe. The ancient Indians believed that the innermost depths of the soul could be revealed through the practice of self-expression.

The practice of self-expression in ancient India was based on the principles of Tantra, which is a philosophy that seeks to unite the individual with the divine and to explore the depths of the soul. Through the art of self-expression, individuals were able to explore their creativity and innermost thoughts, as well as learn about their true nature.

In ancient India, the practice of self-expression was highly valued as a way of understanding and improving oneself. It was believed that the practice of self-expression could help one to gain insight into their own emotions and thoughts, and to gain a better understanding of their own inner desires. It was also believed that through the practice of self-expression, one could learn to better control their emotions and thoughts, and to become more aware of the world around them.

The ancient Indians believed that the practice of self-expression could help to bring about harmony in the individual's life. Through the practice of self-expression, one could learn to accept their emotions and thoughts, and to better understand how they were affecting their lives.

It was also believed that by expressing oneself, one could learn to better communicate with others, which could lead to better relationships and understanding.

The practice of self-expression in ancient India took many forms. It could involve writing, drawing, painting, and the performance of certain rituals. Individuals were also known to practice yoga and meditation as a form of self-expression. Through the practice of these activities, individuals could explore their innermost thoughts and feelings, and gain insight into their true nature.

The practice of self-expression in ancient India was also used to bring about healing. Through the practice of self-expression, individuals could gain a deeper understanding of their own emotions and thoughts, as well as better insight into how they were affecting their lives. It was believed that by expressing their emotions and thoughts in a creative way, individuals could gain a better understanding of themselves, and thus help to bring about healing in their lives.

The practice of self-expression in ancient India was an important part of life. It was believed that through the practice of self-expression, individuals could gain insight into their true nature, and become more aware of the world around them. The practice of self-expression could also help to bring about healing and better understanding. Through the practice of self-expression, individuals could learn to accept their emotions and thoughts, and to better understand how they were affecting their lives.

CHAPTER LXIII

The Nature of Beauty

The concept of beauty in ancient India was far more complex and nuanced than we can imagine today. It was not simply a matter of physical appearance or of adhering to certain standards of perfection. Rather, beauty encompassed a much deeper meaning and was seen as an expression of the divine. In ancient India, beauty was seen as a reflection of the spiritual essence of the individual, reflecting the inner truth of each individual's life.

The ancient Indians believed that beauty was an expression of the soul's journey towards perfection. It was considered to be a reflection of the inner divinity that was present within each person. Ancient texts such as the Upanishads, the Bhagavad Gita, and the Mahabharata, all speak of beauty as being an expression of the inner truth of the individual. The Mahabharata, for example, speaks of beauty as an expression of the soul's journey towards perfection. It states that, "The soul is the source of beauty, and beauty is the source of happiness."

The ancient Indians believed that beauty was not a static concept but rather something that could be developed and enhanced through spiritual practices. This could be done through practices such as yoga, meditation, and the cultivation of virtue. It was believed that the practice of these spiritual disciplines would help to bring the individual closer to the divine, thus enhancing the beauty within them.

The ancient Indians also believed that beauty was linked to the concept of truth or Satya. According to this belief, it was believed that beauty was a reflection of the truth within each individual. It was also believed that beauty was linked to one's moral character and could be enhanced through the practice of virtue and ethical behaviour.

The Indian culture also placed great emphasis on the concept of beauty in its art and architecture. The ancient Indian temples and monuments were all built with the intent of reflecting the inner beauty of the soul. These structures were filled with intricate carvings and sculptures of gods and goddesses that were intended to capture the essence of beauty and harmony.

The ancient Indians also believed that beauty was linked to the concept of dharma. Dharma refers to one's duty or moral code as prescribed by the law of the universe. It was believed that by adhering to the laws of dharma, one could cultivate the inner beauty within them.

In conclusion, it is clear that the nature of beauty in ancient India was far more complex and nuanced than we can imagine today. It was not simply a matter of physical appearance or of adhering to certain standards of perfection. Rather, beauty was seen as an expression of the divine and as a reflection of the inner truth of the individual. It was believed that beauty could be enhanced through spiritual practices and by adhering to the principles of dharma. Finally, beauty was also linked to the concept of truth and was seen as being an expression of one's moral character and ethical behavior.

CHAPTER LXIV

The Principles of Aesthetics

The ancient Indian civilization was an incredibly rich and diverse culture, with a deep and profound understanding of the aesthetic and spiritual aspects of life. Ancient India was a land of beauty, art, and philosophy, and its aesthetic principles have been an inspiration to many cultures throughout the centuries.

The ancient Indian aesthetics were based on the concept of Rasa, which is the essence of life and beauty in each individual. This concept was developed by the Indian philosopher and poet, Bharata Muni, and his work, the Natyashastra, is still the most comprehensive treatise on aesthetics. The Natyashastra was compiled by Bharata Muni during the period of the Gupta Empire in India and it details the eight fundamental aspects of Rasa: Shringara (Love), Hasya (Humor), Karuna (Pathos), Raudra (Anger), Vira (Heroism), Bhayanaka (Fear), Bibhatsa (Disgust), and Adbhuta (Wonder).

The principles of aesthetics in ancient India also laid great emphasis on the importance of harmony, balance, and symmetry in art and architecture. This is evident in the architecture of the Mauryan and Gupta empires, which featured intricate designs and elaborate decorations. The ancient Indian aesthetics also placed great importance on the use of color, texture, and light to create a beautiful and harmonious environment.

The principles of aesthetics in ancient India were also heavily influenced by the philosophy of the Upanishads and the Bhagavad Gita. Indian philosophy is based on the concept of Brahman, which is the ultimate reality, and all other things in the universe are manifestations of this ultimate reality. The Upanishads and the Bhagavad Gita both emphasize the importance of understanding one's own self, and achieving harmony and balance in life. This philosophy is echoed in ancient Indian aesthetics, which emphasize harmony, balance, and symmetry in art and architecture.

The principles of aesthetics in ancient India were also heavily influenced by the concept of Dharma, which is the universal law of truth and righteousness. Dharma is believed to be the basic law of life, and it is essential for maintaining harmony and balance in the universe. Dharma teaches us to act with integrity and compassion, and to be mindful of our actions and their consequences. This is reflected in the ancient Indian aesthetics, which place an emphasis on the importance of balance and harmony in art and architecture.

The principles of aesthetics in ancient India were also strongly influenced by the concept of Yoga, which is a practice of physical and mental discipline. Yoga is believed to help attain inner balance and harmony, and it has been practiced in India for thousands of years. The principles of aesthetics in ancient India were also heavily influenced by the practices of meditation and contemplation, which help to cultivate a deeper understanding of one's self and bring about inner peace.

Overall, the principles of aesthetics in ancient India were based on the concepts of Rasa, Dharma, and Yoga, and have been an inspiration to many cultures throughout the centuries. They emphasize the importance of balance, harmony, and symmetry in art and architecture, as well as the importance of understanding one's own self and cultivating inner peace. Understanding and appreciating the principles of aesthetics in ancient India can help to create a more beautiful and harmonious environment in our lives today.

CHAPTER LXV

The Art of Living in Harmony

The art of living in harmony is an ancient Indian concept that has been practiced for centuries. In ancient India, harmony was seen as a way of life and was considered essential for achieving a balanced and fulfilling life. The ancient Indian sages believed that harmony was the key to inner peace and happiness, and it was through the practice of harmonious living that one could achieve success and contentment.

In ancient India, the art of living in harmony was based on the principles of dharma, or righteousness. Dharma consists of five core values: truth, non-violence, contentment, self-control, and non-attachment. These five values were seen as essential for achieving a balanced and harmonious life. For example, truth was seen as the foundation for all relationships and was essential for maintaining harmony. Non-violence was seen as an essential part of the social order and was essential for maintaining peace and stability. Contentment was seen as essential for achieving inner peace and happiness. Self-control was seen as essential for developing a sound mind and body. And non-attachment was seen as essential for achieving freedom and liberation.

The practice of living in harmony was seen as essential for achieving success in all aspects of life. In ancient India, it was believed that harmony was the key to achieving success in business, relationships, and spiritual endeavors. The practice of living in harmony was seen as essential for achieving success in all areas of life.

The ancient Indian sages also believed that living in harmony was the key to achieving physical health and well-being. Ancient Indian texts such as the Upanishads, Bhagavad Gita, and Yoga Sutras, describe how living in harmony was essential for achieving physical health and well-being. For example, the practice of yoga was seen as an essential part of living in harmony, as it was believed to help balance the body, mind, and spirit.

In addition to physical health, the practice of living in harmony was also believed to help achieve emotional, mental, and spiritual health. Ancient Indian texts such as the Upanishads, Bhagavad Gita, and Yoga Sutras, describe how living in harmony was essential for achieving emotional, mental, and spiritual health. Ancient Indian texts also describe the importance of meditation in achieving greater harmony and balance.

The practice of living in harmony was also seen as essential for achieving success in all aspects of life. Ancient Indian texts such as the Upanishads, Bhagavad Gita, and Yoga Sutras, describe how living in harmony was essential for achieving success in all areas of life. For example, the practice of non-attachment was seen as essential for achieving success in business and relationships, while the practice of self-control was seen as essential for achieving success in spiritual endeavors.

The practice of living in harmony was also seen as essential for achieving inner peace and happiness. Ancient Indian texts such as the Upanishads, Bhagavad Gita, and Yoga Sutras, describe how living in harmony was essential for achieving inner peace and happiness. The practice of living in harmony was seen as essential for developing a sound mind and body, as well as for achieving liberation from suffering.

In conclusion, the art of living in harmony is an ancient Indian concept that has been practiced for centuries. The practice of living in harmony was seen as essential for achieving physical, emotional, mental, and spiritual health, as well as for achieving success in all areas of life. The practice of living in harmony was also seen as essential for achieving inner peace and happiness, as well as for achieving liberation from suffering. The principles of dharma, or righteousness, were seen as essential for achieving a balanced and harmonious life.

CHAPTER LXVI

The Power of Friendship

Friendship has always been an important part of Indian culture. Ancient India was a time when people valued friendship and relationships over material possessions. In ancient India, friendship was seen as a powerful force that could bring people together, regardless of their social or economic status.

The power of friendship in ancient India was so strong that it created an unspoken bond between people. It was believed that friends could help each other in times of need and provide emotional support. Friends could also be trusted to keep secrets, provide advice, and offer comfort and security.

In ancient India, friendship was seen as a source of strength and courage. It was believed that two friends could be stronger than an army of ten thousand men. This was because, with the power of friendship, two people could support each other and provide strength and courage when needed.

In addition, friendship was seen as a way to build strong relationships between people. Ancient Indian society was based on the concept of "vasudhaiva kutumbakam", which means "the world is one family". This concept is still relevant today, as it emphasizes the importance of treating everyone as if they were family and creating strong bonds of friendship between people.

In ancient India, friendship was also seen as a way to gain knowledge and understanding. Friends could discuss different aspects of life and help each other develop wisdom. This was especially true for students, who could gain knowledge and wisdom from their peers.

Friendship in ancient India was not just limited to humans, but also extended to animals. In the Mahabharata, Arjuna is described as having a strong bond with his chariot horses. This bond was so strong that the horses were willing to sacrifice their lives for Arjuna in battle. This shows that friendship was seen as a powerful force that could even influence animals.

Finally, friendship in ancient India was seen as a way to bring peace and harmony to the world. Friendships could help reduce conflicts and build bridges between different communities and cultures. This is why ancient Indian rulers often used the power of friendship to bring peace to their kingdoms and to promote understanding between different people.

The power of friendship in ancient India was so strong that it still influences Indian culture and society today. Friendships are still valued and seen as a source of strength, courage, wisdom, and understanding. People still turn to their friends for advice and support, and friendships are still seen as a way to bring peace and harmony to the world.

CHAPTER LXVII

The Practice of Compassion

Compassion is a term that is used to describe an emotion of sympathy and understanding for the suffering of others. In ancient India, the practice of compassion was deeply rooted in the culture and was considered an essential part of being a human being. Compassion was seen as a way to show respect and kindness to others, and was a way of expressing love and affirming the inherent value of all life.

In the Vedas, the oldest scriptures of Hinduism, compassion was seen as one of the most important virtues. The Vedas taught that all living creatures should be treated with kindness and respect, and that compassion was a key element in leading a moral life. Compassion was seen as one of the four divine qualities that humans should strive to practice in order to live a life of righteousness.

In the Bhagavad Gita, a scripture that is considered to be the most important Hindu text, compassion is seen as an essential part of the path to spiritual enlightenment. The Gita teaches that we should be kind and compassionate to all living creatures, and that it is our duty to help those in need. Compassion is seen as a way of connecting with God, as it shows our willingness to rise above our own selfish desires and to serve the greater good.

In the Upanishads, another set of ancient texts, compassion is seen as one of the primary virtues that humans should strive to cultivate. The Upanishads teach that we should have compassion for all living beings, and that it is our duty to help those in need. Compassion is seen as an essential element in leading a moral life, and is seen as a way to cultivate inner peace and contentment.

Compassion was also an important part of Buddhism. The Buddhist scriptures, the Pali Canon, teach that we should develop compassion for all living beings and that it is an essential part of the path to enlightenment. The scriptures also teach that we should practice loving-kindness towards all living beings, and that we should be compassionate and forgiving even in the face of adversity.

In conclusion, compassion was an important part of ancient India. The Vedas, the Bhagavad Gita, and the Upanishads all taught that we should have compassion for all living beings, and that it is our duty to help those in need. Compassion was seen as an essential element in leading a moral life, and was a way to cultivate inner peace and contentment. The Buddhist scriptures taught that we should develop compassion for all living beings and that it is an essential part of the path to enlightenment. Compassion was, and still is, an essential part of Indian culture and is an important part of the practice of wisdom of lost Bharat.

CHAPTER LXVIII

The Wisdom of Joy

The ancient Indian sages, seers, and rishis have been credited with imparting profound wisdom on the subject of joy. According to ancient Indian philosophy, joy is something that comes from within. It is not dependent on external factors or circumstances, but rather on our inner state of being. Joy is a state of spiritual bliss, a deep sense of contentment, and a feeling of connection to something greater than ourselves.

The ancient Indian seers understood that joy is the key to living a balanced, meaningful life. They believed that joy was the path to fulfillment, and that it was essential for attaining enlightenment. Joy was seen as a source of inner strength and resilience, enabling us to face our challenges with courage and grace.

The ancient Indian sages taught that joy is not something that can be achieved through material possessions or external achievements. Instead, they believed that joy comes from within, and is the result of the cultivation of inner peace and harmony. The ancient Indian seers advocated a life of moderation, which was designed to bring balance and joy to all aspects of life. They believed that a life of moderation was essential for promoting joy and contentment.

According to ancient Indian wisdom, joy is a state of being that is accessible to all. The ancient Indian seers taught that joy is something that can be cultivated through mindful practice and the observance of certain principles. For example, they taught that developing a sense of gratitude was essential for cultivating joy. They also taught that cultivating compassion, kindness, and forgiveness was essential for experiencing true joy.

The ancient Indian sages understood that joy is not something that can be forced or achieved through the acquisition of material possessions. Instead, they believed that joy can only be experienced when we are truly present in the moment and living our lives with an attitude of gratitude and appreciation.

The ancient Indian wisdom on joy emphasized the importance of living a life of balance and harmony. They taught that joy is not dependent on external circumstances, but rather on our inner state of being. They believed that true joy comes from within, and is the result of cultivating inner peace and harmony.

The ancient Indian sages also taught that joy is something that can be shared. They believed that joy was something that could be experienced not only within ourselves, but also with those around us. They taught that joy can be shared through acts of kindness and compassion, and through creating meaningful relationships with others.

The ancient Indian sages emphasized the importance of living a life of joy and contentment. They taught that joy is something that can be cultivated through mindful practice and the observance of certain principles. They believed that joy is something that can be experienced both within ourselves and with those around us. They also believed that joy is something that can be shared through acts of kindness and compassion, and through creating meaningful relationships with others.

CHAPTER LXIX

The Nature of Love

Love is an emotion that has been celebrated since antiquity in many cultures and societies. Ancient India was no exception. Indian scriptures, poetry, and literature from the Vedic period to the Gupta period speak of love in various forms, from divine love to passionate love between two people. The Nature of Love in Ancient India is therefore an interesting and complex topic.

In Vedic literature, love is seen as an emotion that transcends all boundaries. It is an emotion of divine origin, something that unites all beings, regardless of their caste, class, gender, or religion. This is seen in the Rig Veda where love is described as being like the sun, shining on all with the same intensity. The Upanishads also speak of love in a similar way, as a unifying force that binds all of creation together.

In ancient India, love was also seen as a source of strength and power. Love was often used as a metaphor for the power of spiritual enlightenment. In the Bhagavad Gita, Krishna talks of the power of love between two people as a force that can bring peace and contentment. In the Mahabharata, the Pandavas are compared to the power of love, as their love for each other is what makes them stronger than their enemies.

The Nature of Love in Ancient India also includes the idea of passionate love between two people. In the Ramayana, the love between Rama and Sita is portrayed as a passionate romance. In the Mahabharata, the love between Draupadi and Arjuna is portrayed as a passionate relationship as well. This type of love is seen as a source of strength, as it allows two people to be connected on a deeper level and to support each other through difficult times.

The Nature of Love in Ancient India also includes the concept of love between a guru and a disciple. This type of relationship is seen as a special bond of trust and respect between two people. The guru is seen as a teacher and mentor, while the disciple is seen as a student who learns from the guru. This type of relationship is seen as a source of strength and guidance, and it is often seen as a source of spiritual enlightenment.

Finally, the Nature of Love in Ancient India also includes the idea of love between two Gods. This type of love is seen as a source of divine power, as it is seen as the source of all knowledge and understanding. This type of love is often seen as a source of protection and guidance, and it is seen as a source of spiritual enlightenment.

In conclusion, Love in Ancient India is a complex and multi-faceted emotion. It is seen as a source of strength, power, and divine guidance. It is seen as a unifying force that binds all of creation together, and it is seen as a source of spiritual enlightenment. Love in Ancient India is an emotion that transcends all boundaries, and it is an emotion that is celebrated and cherished.

CHAPTER LXX

The Path of Gratitude

The Path of Gratitude has been an integral part of ancient Indian culture since time immemorial. In India, the spiritual practice of gratitude has been passed down through generations, and is a cornerstone of many religious and spiritual traditions. The concept of gratitude has been deeply embedded in the way of life of India's people, and is seen as an important part of the journey towards enlightenment.

The Path of Gratitude is not only a spiritual practice, but also a way of living. It is about recognizing and appreciating the beauty of life and all that it has to offer. It is about acknowledging that life is precious and we should be grateful for the small things that bring us joy. Gratitude is about taking the time to stop and appreciate the beauty of life and all that it has to offer.

The ancient Indian scriptures, such as the Upanishads, Bhagavad Gita and Vedas, lay out the importance of gratitude in its teachings. These scriptures offer guidance on how to live a life of gratitude and appreciation, and how to use it as a tool to reach enlightenment.

The Path of Gratitude is about being mindful of the blessings and joy that life has to offer. It is about being thankful for the good things that come our way, and being mindful of the bad. It is about learning to accept the things that we cannot change, and appreciating the things that we can.

The Path of Gratitude is also about recognizing the interconnectedness of all things. It encourages us to recognize that we are all part of a larger universe and that everything is connected. By taking the time to appreciate the beauty of our world, we can learn to be grateful for what we have and for the people we share it with.

The Path of Gratitude encourages us to be mindful of our thoughts and words. It teaches us to be mindful of our actions and how they affect others. It also encourages us to be mindful of our relationships and how we can act in ways that bring out the best in each other.

The Path of Gratitude is a powerful practice that can help us to become more aware of the beauty and joy in our lives. It can help us to appreciate the good that comes our way, and to have a greater appreciation for the people and things in our lives. By recognizing the interconnectedness of all things, we can learn to be more grateful for the blessings that life has to offer.

The practice of gratitude is an essential part of the Indian spiritual tradition. By taking the time to appreciate the beauty of life and all that it has to offer, we can learn to be grateful for the small things that bring us joy. The Path of Gratitude is about recognizing and appreciating the beauty of life and all that it has to offer, and knowing that life is precious.

8. The Science of Nature

The Science of Nature is a holistic approach to understanding the natural environment and how it interacts with humans. It involves the observation and study of the physical, biological, and spiritual aspects of the natural world, emphasizing the power of nature, the practice of observation, the understanding of natural cycles, the principles of ecology, the art of sustainable living, the power of indigenous wisdom, the practice of natural medicine, the wisdom of herbalism, the nature of plant spirituality, and the path of rituals. By studying the science of nature, we can gain a deeper appreciation and understanding of the natural world and our place within it.

CHAPTER LXXI

The Power of Nature

The ancient Indians believed in the power of nature and its ability to influence their lives. They believed that the natural world was an extension of the divine, and that it held the secrets to life. They understood that nature was both a source of sustenance and a source of danger. It was a source of nourishment, providing food, water, and shelter, while it also held the potential for destruction in the form of floods, drought, and other natural disasters.

The ancient Indians' reverence for nature was reflected in their religious and spiritual beliefs. They believed that all of nature was interconnected, and that humans were part of an intricate web of life. They believed that their actions could have a profound effect on the natural world, and that their relationship with nature was a sacred one.

The ancient Indians also used the power of nature to heal and protect. They used plants and herbs for medicinal purposes, and believed that certain plants had the power to ward off disease and negative energy. They also believed in the power of certain animals, such as tigers and lions, to bring luck and protection.

The ancient Indians also believed in the power of certain objects to bring good luck. They believed that certain stones, crystals, and metals could be used to attract wealth, health, and happiness. They also believed that certain symbols, such as the swastika, held special meaning and power. They used these symbols to ward off evil, attract good luck, and bring success.

The ancient Indians also believed in the power of nature to shape the destiny of a person. They believed that certain events, such as floods or earthquakes, were signs that the gods were displeased and that the person should take steps to make amends. They also believed that certain animals, such as cows and horses, could be used to predict the future.

The ancient Indians also believed that certain places held special power. They believed that certain mountains, rivers, and forests were the abode of gods and goddesses, and that these places held the power to bring good luck and protection. They also believed that certain lakes and springs had the power to heal and purify.

The ancient Indians believed that nature was both a source of sustenance and a source of danger. They respected and revered nature, and believed in its power to influence their lives. They used it to heal, protect, and bring good luck, and to shape their destiny. The power of nature was an integral part of the ancient Indian culture, and is still respected today.

CHAPTER LXXII

The Practice of Observation

Observation is an important practice in ancient India, as it is in many cultures. It is a practice of paying attention to the world around us, noticing subtle details and perceiving connections that we might not have noticed without taking the time to observe. Ancient Indian texts such as the Upanishads, Bhagavad Gita, and Mahabharata reveal that observation was an important part of spiritual practice in the country.

The Upanishads, which are collections of philosophical and spiritual teachings, emphasize the importance of observation. In the Brihadaranyaka Upanishad, one of the oldest Upanishads, it is stated that "The wise man, in order to know Brahman, must observe." Brahman is the ultimate reality in Hinduism and it is believed that by observing the world, we can gain insight into this reality. The Katha Upanishad, another ancient text, also states that "Those who observe, who are devoted to their studies, and who are ever inquiring, reach the highest goal." This emphasizes that observation is essential for spiritual growth and understanding.

The Bhagavad Gita, one of the most important Hindu texts, also mentions the importance of observation. In the Gita, Krishna tells Arjuna that in order to understand the truth, he must observe the world. He states that, "Those who are established in the practice of observing and perceiving the truth, who are liberated from all attachments and aversions, who have conquered their senses, and who are devoted to me, they are the ones who attain the supreme goal." This reveals that observation is essential for attaining liberation and understanding the truth.

The Mahabharata, an epic poem, also mentions the importance of observation. In the Mahabharata, Yudhishthira, the eldest of the five Pandava brothers, states that "One should observe the world with care, for it is the source of knowledge." He also tells his brothers that "By observing the world, one can learn and grow." This emphasizes that observation is essential for learning and growth.

Observation is also an important part of meditation in ancient India. Meditation was often used to achieve higher states of consciousness and spiritual enlightenment. Meditation is also used to observe the mind and the body, as well as one's thoughts and feelings. In the Yoga Sutras of Patanjali, one of the most important texts on yoga and meditation, it is said that "Through observation and contemplation, one can understand the true nature of things." This reveals that observation is essential for understanding the true nature of reality.

In conclusion, observation is an important practice in ancient India. The Upanishads, Bhagavad Gita, and Mahabharata all emphasize the importance of observation for gaining insight into reality and achieving spiritual growth. Additionally, meditation is often used as a way of observing the mind and body and understanding the true nature of things. Thus, observation is an essential part of spiritual practice in ancient India, and it is still practiced today.

CHAPTER LXXIII

The Nature of Natural Cycles

The ancient Indian culture had a deep understanding of natural cycles and the importance of being in tune with them. From the four yugas that cyclically form a basic timeline for events and developments in the universe, to the cycle of the seasons and the cycles of the day and night, ancient Indians recognised the importance of being in tune with the natural world in order to live in harmony with it.

The ancient Indians had a great reverence for the natural cycles, believing them to be a reflection of the divine. This reverence was expressed in the way they lived their lives, in the rituals they performed and in the stories they told. The four yugas, which form the basis of the Hindu calendar, illustrate this reverence for the cyclical nature of time. These four yugas, the Satya Yuga, the Treta Yuga, the Dvapara Yuga and the Kali Yuga, are believed to be four successive periods of time in which human values and lifestyles vary. While the cycle of the four yugas is believed to take several thousand years, the cycle of the seasons and the cycle of the day and night are much shorter, but equally important.

The cycle of the seasons is an important part of ancient Indian culture, as it is linked to many of the festivals and ceremonies celebrated throughout the year. The four seasons, spring, summer, autumn and winter, were seen as having their own spiritual significance and represented different aspects of nature. The cycle of the seasons was also believed to be a reflection of the four yugas, with each season being associated with one of the yugas. In addition, the harvesting of crops and the changing of the weather were seen as a reflection of the cycle of the seasons, and were celebrated as part of the rituals associated with festivals.

The cycle of the day and night was also seen as a reflection of the divine, and was believed to be an important part of living in harmony with nature. Ancient Indians believed that the cycle of the day and night was linked to the cycle of the four yugas, with each yuga being associated with one of the four time periods. During the Satya Yuga, the day was believed to be associated with peace and harmony, while the night was associated with darkness and ignorance. During the Treta Yuga, the day was associated with knowledge and wisdom, and the night was associated with rest and rejuvenation. During the Dvapara Yuga, the day was associated with activity and productivity, while the night was seen as a time for contemplation and meditation. Finally, during the Kali Yuga, the day was associated with suffering and sorrow, while the night was seen as a time for renewal and hope.

The nature of natural cycles in ancient India was seen as a reflection of the divine, and was a major part of their culture. They believed that living in tune with the cycles of nature was essential for living in harmony with the world. Ancient Indians respected and celebrated the cycle of the seasons and the cycle of the day and night, and saw them as a reflection of the four yugas. This reverence for the cycle of nature was an important part of ancient Indian culture, and is still seen today in the way that many Hindus celebrate the festivals and ceremonies associated with the cycle of the seasons.

CHAPTER LXXIV

The Principles of Ecology

Ecology is the study of the relationship between organisms and their environment and the complex web of interactions that exist between them. In ancient India, ecology was understood in a very holistic and interconnected way, and the principles of ecology were embedded in all aspects of life.

The ancient Indian texts of the Vedas, Upanishads, Smritis, and Puranas, provide insight into the thoughts and practices of the people of the time and the principles of ecology that guided their actions. These scriptures, together with the works of great Indian scientists such as Charaka, Patanjali, Kanada, and Susruta, are essential sources of knowledge on the principles of ecology in ancient India.

One of the most important concepts in the ecology of ancient India was the idea of Prakriti, which refers to the natural state of balance and harmony between the environment and its inhabitants. The idea of Prakriti was based on the belief that everything in nature is connected and that any disruption of this balance could lead to chaos and destruction. This concept was used to explain natural phenomena such as floods, droughts, and other environmental catastrophes.

The principles of ecology in ancient India also included the belief in the interconnectedness of all life. This concept was articulated in the Vedic hymns, which describe how all living beings are connected through a system of natural laws. The Upanishads also speak of the interconnectedness of all things, emphasizing the need to treat all creatures with respect and compassion.

The principles of ecology in ancient India also included the belief that humans should strive to live in harmony with nature. This was expressed in the concept of Dharma, which refers to the moral code of conduct that people should adhere to in order to maintain harmony and balance in the environment. The concept of Dharma was also used to explain why certain actions were beneficial for the environment, such as conservation and the protection of natural resources.

The principles of ecology in ancient India also included the recognition that human activity could have a negative impact on the environment. The Smritis, for example, advised people to practice moderation when it came to activities such as farming, hunting, and fishing. They also warned against deforestation and the destruction of natural habitats.

Finally, the principles of ecology in ancient India also included the belief that humans should respect the earth and its resources. The Puranas spoke of the need to take only what is necessary from the environment and not to waste or abuse natural resources. They stressed the importance of preserving the environment for future generations and warned against the dangers of pollution.

The principles of ecology in ancient India were closely linked to other aspects of life such as religion, philosophy, and science. They were also an important part of the Indian way of life and provided a framework for sustainable living. By understanding and following these principles, people in ancient India were able to create a society that was able to thrive in harmony with nature.

CHAPTER LXXV

The Art of Sustainable Living

The ancient Indian approach to sustainable living is one of the oldest and most unique approaches to sustainability in the world. It goes beyond a simple concept of sustainability, and instead focuses on the holistic approach to living a balanced, harmonious life that respects the environment and recognizes the interconnectedness of all things. This approach, which has been passed down through generations, still resonates today in many aspects of Indian culture and is still practiced in many rural and remote parts of the country.

The most fundamental component of sustainable living in ancient India was the concept of ahimsa, or nonviolence. This concept was based on the belief that all living beings, no matter how small, have a right to life and to be respected. This idea was reflected in everything from the way people treated their animals and plants to the way they interacted with each other. It was believed that if one acted with kindness and compassion towards all creatures, then one could create a harmonious and sustainable environment.

In order to create a sustainable environment, the ancient Indians also paid close attention to the intricate balance between nature and man. This balance was achieved through the practice of prana, or the proper utilization of natural resources. Prana was a complex system of rules, regulations, and guidelines that guided how resources were used and managed. This system was based around the concept that all living creatures were interconnected, and that the harmony of the natural world could be maintained through careful management of resources.

The ancient Indian approach to sustainable living also included the practice of Brahmacharya, which was a way of living that focused on self-control and moderation. This practice emphasized the importance of living a life of moderation and balance. People were encouraged to live within their means, practice contentment with what they had, and to be mindful of their impact on the environment. This practice was based on the belief that a healthy and sustainable environment could be achieved through self-discipline, and that moderation was the key to achieving this balance.

The ancient Indian approach to sustainable living was also based on the concept of Dharma, or the moral law. Dharma was based on the belief that all living beings should act in accordance with the natural laws of the universe, and that those laws should be respected. This concept was reflected in the way the ancient Indians treated their animals, the way they interacted with each other, and the way they treated their environment. It was believed that if one acted in accordance with Dharma, then one could create a harmonious and sustainable environment.

The ancient Indian approach to sustainable living was also based on the concept of Satya, or truth. This concept was based on the idea that truth was the foundation of all relationships, both with the environment and with each other. It was believed that if one acted in accordance with truth, then one could create a sustainable and harmonious environment.

The ancient Indian approach to sustainable living is still relevant today, and it can provide us with valuable insight into how we can create a sustainable environment. By following the principles of ahimsa, prana, Brahmacharya, Dharma, and Satya, we can create a balanced and harmonious environment that respects the interconnectedness of all things. This approach can help us to create sustainable communities and can help us to live in harmony with nature.

CHAPTER LXXVI

The Power of Indigenous Wisdom

India is a country steeped in ancient wisdom and knowledge. From yoga and meditation, to Ayurveda and Vedic science, the wisdom of India's indigenous and spiritual traditions has been a cornerstone of Indian culture for thousands of years. This wisdom has been passed down through generations, forming the basis of the country's philosophical, spiritual and cultural heritage.

The power of ancient Indian wisdom lies in its ability to provide unparalleled insight into the complexity of the human experience. From understanding the nuances of relationships and dealing with difficult emotions, to providing guidance on how to live a meaningful, purposeful life, the wisdom of India's ancient traditions has been instrumental in helping countless individuals find peace and enlightenment.

At the heart of India's ancient wisdom is the concept of dharma – the idea that each individual has a unique and integral role to play in the world. Dharma has been an integral part of Indian culture for thousands of years, informing an individual's sense of duty and morality. This concept was so deeply ingrained in the Indian psyche that it was often used as a way to determine a person's caste, or social standing.

Another key concept of Indian wisdom is that of karma, or the law of cause and effect. The idea is that every action has an equal and opposite reaction, and that one's current life is the result of their past actions. This concept of karma is often used to explain why some people experience suffering or difficulty in their lives, and why some people appear to have an easier life than others.

The wisdom of India's indigenous traditions also places great emphasis on the power of meditation and mindfulness. Meditation is seen as a way to connect with one's true self and to gain insight into the deeper meaning of life. Meditation is believed to help individuals become more aware and mindful of their thoughts, feelings and actions, leading to greater inner peace.

The wisdom of India's ancient traditions is also important in understanding the power of compassion. Compassion is seen as a way of understanding the suffering of others and taking on the responsibility of helping alleviate their suffering. Compassion is seen as a way of showing respect and honoring the life of another, and as a way of connecting to the divine.

The power of ancient Indian wisdom lies in its ability to provide unparalleled insight into the complexity of the human experience. From understanding the nuances of relationships and dealing with difficult emotions, to providing guidance on how to live a meaningful, purposeful life, the wisdom of India's ancient traditions has been instrumental in helping countless individuals find peace and enlightenment. This wisdom has been passed down through generations, forming the basis of the country's philosophical, spiritual and cultural heritage. As such, it is no wonder that the wisdom of India's ancient traditions still holds great relevance today.

CHAPTER LXXVII

The Practice of Natural Medicine

The practice of natural medicine in ancient India dates back thousands of years. It was a holistic approach to healing, involving a combination of physical, mental, spiritual, and environmental factors. In this system, health was seen as a balance between the body, mind, and spirit, and illness was thought to be caused by an imbalance in this balance.

Natural medicine was used to treat a variety of ailments, and there were many methods used. Herbal remedies were used in the form of teas, decoctions, and poultices. Ayurveda, the ancient system of Indian medicine, was also widely practiced. This system used a variety of herbal remedies, as well as diet, lifestyle, and exercise to achieve balance and health.

Acupuncture, massage, and other forms of bodywork were also used to treat a variety of physical and mental conditions. These practices were believed to stimulate the flow of energy, called prana, throughout the body and restore balance. They were also used to relieve pain, reduce inflammation, and support the body's natural healing process.

Yoga and meditation were also used as a form of natural medicine. These practices were believed to reduce stress and tension, calm the mind, and restore balance. Meditation was used to increase self-awareness and cultivate inner peace, which was believed to be beneficial for health.

In addition to these practices, natural medicine also included the use of plants, minerals, and animal products.

Plants were used to make herbal remedies, and minerals, such as sulfur and copper, were used to treat a variety of ailments. Animal products, such as snakes, were also used to make medicines.

The practice of natural medicine in ancient India was a holistic approach to healing that focused on restoring balance between the body, mind, and spirit. It was believed that an imbalance in any of these areas could lead to illness. A variety of remedies, including herbal remedies, bodywork, yoga, meditation, and the use of plants and minerals, were used to restore balance and health. This system of medicine was practiced for centuries, and it is still used today in many parts of the world.

CHAPTER LXXVIII

The Wisdom of Herbalism

Herbalism is an ancient practice that has been used in India for thousands of years. It is based on the belief that plants have medicinal properties that can be used to treat a wide range of ailments. Herbalism has been an integral part of Indian culture since ancient times, and it is still widely practiced today.

The use of herbs and plants for healing is a very old practice in India. Indian Ayurveda, a holistic system of medicine, has been in use since ancient times. Ayurveda is based on the belief that plants contain medicinal properties that can be used to treat a variety of ailments. Ayurvedic practitioners use herbs, spices, and other plant-based substances to treat physical and emotional ailments.

The ancient Vedic texts, such as the Rig Veda, also mention the use of herbs for medicinal purposes. These ancient texts provide detailed descriptions of various plants, their properties, and how they can be used to treat various ailments. This knowledge was passed down from generation to generation, and is still used today.

In ancient India, herbalism was widely practiced by both men and women. Women were often more knowledgeable about the use of herbs, as they were usually in charge of domestic tasks such as cooking and preparing medicines. Women also used herbs to treat their own illnesses, as well as those of their family members.

Herbal remedies were considered to be more effective than modern medicines, as they were believed to be more natural and gentle on the body. Herbs were also believed to be more affordable, as they could be grown in one's own garden or purchased from the local market.

Herbalism was not only used to treat physical ailments, but also emotional and spiritual problems. Herbal remedies were believed to be able to bring balance and harmony to an individual's life. Herbalists believed that the different properties of each herb could be used to treat a variety of ailments, from depression to insomnia.

The ancient practice of herbalism is still widely practiced in India today. Herbalists often blend different herbs together to create herbal remedies that can be used to treat a wide range of ailments. Many of these remedies are thought to have been passed down through the generations, and are still used today.

Herbalism is a powerful and ancient practice that is still practiced in India today. It is believed to be an effective form of natural healing, as it is based on the belief that plants contain medicinal properties that can be used to treat a variety of ailments. Herbalists believe that by using herbs, spices, and other plant-based substances, they can bring balance and harmony to an individual's life. Herbalism is an integral part of Indian culture, and is a practice that has been used for thousands of years.

CHAPTER LXXIX

The Nature of Plant Spirituality

The ancient Indian spiritual tradition has long been associated with the reverence of plants and the environment. Plant spirituality is deeply rooted in the Hindu, Buddhist and Jain religious traditions and is reflected in many of their scriptures and teachings. This reverence for plants and the environment is also evident in the Vedic culture and is a central element of Indian culture today.

The ancient Indian spiritual tradition has long held that plants possess their own energy, or spirit, and that these plants can be used to connect with the divine. This is a belief that has been passed down through generations and is still practiced today in many parts of India. For example, in the north-western regions of India, many sacred plants are still used for religious ceremonies and rituals.

In the Vedic texts, plants are described as having their own life force and spiritual energy, which can be used for healing and spiritual growth. The Vedas describe plants as being part of the natural world, and as such, they are believed to have the power to heal and transform. Plants are also seen as a source of nourishment, and their use in religious ceremonies and rituals is thought to bring the divine spirit into the lives of those who partake in them.

In the Hindu spiritual tradition, plant spirits are often associated with the gods and goddesses of the Vedic pantheon. Plants are seen as a direct connection to the gods and goddesses and are used to invoke their blessings and protection. For example, Tulsi, a sacred plant in Hinduism, is associated with the goddess Lakshmi, who symbolizes abundance and prosperity. Similarly, the leaves of the Ashoka tree are associated with the god Shiva, who is the destroyer and regenerator of the universe.

In the Buddhist tradition, plants are seen as a source of healing and transformation. They are believed to possess healing properties and can be used to help balance the body, mind and spirit. The Buddha himself was said to have meditated amongst the trees and plants of the forest and to have received healing from them. Plants are also seen as a source of spiritual nourishment, and the use of plants in religious ceremonies and rituals is thought to help one connect with the divine.

The Jain tradition also has a strong connection to plants and their spiritual energy. Jains believe that plants possess the power to transform and heal, and that they can be used to connect with the divine. They also believe that the use of plants in religious ceremonies and rituals can help one to become more attuned with the divine.

The Nature of Plant Spirituality in ancient India is a complex and fascinating one, rooted in a deep reverence for the environment and the plants that inhabit it. It is a belief that has been passed down through generations and is still practiced today in many parts of India. This reverence for plants and the environment is evident in the Vedic culture and is a central element of Indian culture today. The use of plants in religious ceremonies and rituals is believed to bring the divine spirit into the lives of those who partake in them, and to help one to become more attuned with the divine.

CHAPTER LXXX

The Path of Rituals

Rituals in ancient India have been an integral part of life for centuries. It is believed that rituals were first introduced to the people of India by the Vedic civilization and were then passed down from generation to generation. Throughout the centuries, these rituals have been used as a way to express one's devotion to the divine, to honor ancestors, and to strengthen relationships between individuals and communities.

In ancient India, rituals were believed to be a means to appease the gods and goddesses, to seek their blessings and protection, and to ensure a successful life. The rituals were often performed in temples, and although they varied in complexity and duration, they generally involved offerings and prayers to the gods. The most common offerings were food, clothing, jewelry, flowers, incense, and coins. Some rituals were performed to mark important events in a person's life, such as birth, marriage, and death, while others were performed to mark seasonal changes or to celebrate festivals.

The Vedas, the ancient scriptures of India, contain various rituals that are still performed in Hindu temples today. These rituals are known as puja, and involve the chanting of mantras, the offering of food, flowers, and incense, and the lighting of candles and lamps. Puja is usually performed in the presence of an image of the deity, which may be a statue or painting, and is often accompanied by music and dance.

In addition to puja, there are other rituals that are associated with the worship of the gods and goddesses. These include yajna, which is a ritual offering made to the gods, and homa, which is a fire ceremony. Both of these rituals involve the offering of ghee, milk, and other grains and flowers to the flames. Other rituals include the chanting of mantras, the offering of flowers and incense, and the recitation of hymns and scriptures.

Rituals in ancient India were not only performed in temples, but also in homes. During festivals and special occasions, family members would gather together to perform rituals such as puja, yajna, homa, and chanting of mantras. These rituals were believed to bring good luck and prosperity to the family, and to bring the family closer to the divine.

Rituals in ancient India were not simply a way to show devotion to the gods and goddesses, but were also a way to bring people together and to express the importance of the family and community. They were a way for people to connect with their past and to form strong bonds with each other. The rituals were a way to honor the gods and goddesses and to give thanks for the blessings that were bestowed upon them.

The path of rituals in ancient India has been a source of wisdom and knowledge for centuries, and is still practiced today in many parts of the world. It is a reminder of the importance of honoring the divine and of the importance of family and community. The wisdom of these rituals is still relevant today, and can be used as a source of guidance and inspiration.

9. The Path of Spirituality

The Path of Spirituality is a journey of self-discovery and connection to the divine. It is a practice of exploring the power of meditation, mindfulness, and enlightenment, as well as the principles of self-realization and the art of contemplation. Intuition, spiritual inquiry, and the wisdom of the heart can all be cultivated through this path, as well as the power of love and compassion. Finally, the ultimate goal is to surrender to the divine and allow yourself to be guided along the path of spiritual growth and connection.

CHAPTER LXXXI

The Power of Meditation

Meditation has been a part of Indian life and culture for thousands of years. It is an integral part of Hinduism, Buddhism, Jainism and other Indian philosophical systems. The practice of meditating has been used to cultivate greater inner peace, gain higher levels of consciousness, and gain insight into the true nature of reality. The power of meditation in ancient India is one of the most powerful forces in its culture and has been used for centuries to achieve spiritual growth and enlightenment.

The earliest references to meditation are found in the Vedas, a collection of ancient Indian holy texts. In the Vedas, meditation is described as an activity which helps an individual transcend their physical and mental limitations and achieve a higher state of consciousness. It is believed that through meditation, the practitioner can become one with the universal consciousness and gain greater insight into the nature of reality.

Meditation has been used by many great sages and saints throughout India's history. The famous sage Patanjali is credited with creating the Yoga Sutras, which are a collection of teachings on the practice of meditation. Patanjali's teachings laid the foundation for the practice of yoga as we know it today.

The power of meditation in ancient India is also found in the Upanishads, which are a group of ancient texts that discuss the nature of reality and the relationship between the individual and the divine. The Upanishads discuss various meditation techniques such as pranayama (breath control), pratyahara (withdrawal of the senses), dharana (concentration) and dhyana (meditation). These techniques are still used in modern yoga and meditation practice.

The Bhagavad Gita is another ancient Indian text which discusses the power of meditation. In it, Lord Krishna teaches Arjuna, the hero of the Mahabharata, the importance of meditation in order to gain inner peace and insight into the true nature of reality. Lord Krishna also speaks of the power of meditation in attaining the highest state of consciousness, enlightenment, and freedom from suffering.

The power of meditation in ancient India is also found in the teachings of the great Indian sage and spiritual teacher, Adi Shankara. He taught that meditation is the most effective way to attain spiritual knowledge and liberation from the cycle of suffering. He also taught that the power of meditation is the ultimate teacher and that it should be used to gain insight into the ultimate truth.

The power of meditation in ancient India has been used for centuries to cultivate inner peace and spiritual growth. It is an integral part of Hinduism, Buddhism, Jainism and other Indian philosophical systems. Today, the power of meditation is still widely used by many people around the world to gain higher levels of consciousness and achieve greater insight into the true nature of reality.

CHAPTER LXXXII

The Practice of Mindfulness

Mindfulness is a practice that has been around for centuries, and it has been found to be beneficial for a variety of physical and mental health issues. In ancient India, mindfulness was a key part of the spiritual practices of Hinduism, Buddhism, and Jainism. These traditions have been around for centuries, and the practice of mindfulness has been incorporated into them for just as long.

The practice of mindfulness in ancient India was focused on developing an awareness of one's thoughts, feelings, and actions in the present moment. Mindfulness was seen as a way to free oneself from the cycle of suffering and to develop a deeper understanding of the inner self. It was believed that by cultivating mindfulness, one could become more aware of the interconnectedness between the physical and spiritual realms, and ultimately, to enlightenment.

The practice of mindfulness in ancient India was often associated with meditation, although it was also incorporated into other spiritual practices. In yoga, for example, mindful breathing was used to help the practitioner become aware of their inner state and to maintain a sense of calm and clarity. In Jainism, mindfulness was used to cultivate right conduct, as well as to develop a deeper understanding of the interconnectedness between oneself and others.

In order to practice mindfulness in ancient India, there were several techniques that were used. These included paying attention to one's breath, focusing on specific body parts, and paying attention to one's thoughts and feelings without judgment. Mindfulness was also used to observe the environment and to be aware of the interconnectedness between all living beings.

The practice of mindfulness in ancient India was not only beneficial for the individual, but it was also seen as a way to improve the community as a whole. It was believed that by cultivating mindfulness, one could become more aware of their connection to other living beings and the environment, and ultimately, to develop a sense of compassion and respect for all living things.

Mindfulness was also seen as a way to reduce stress and anxiety, as well as to develop better habits and behaviors. It was believed that by being mindful and paying attention to one's thoughts and feelings, one could become more aware of how their actions impacted their environment and those around them. Ultimately, this could lead to greater harmony and balance in one's life.

The practice of mindfulness in ancient India was an important part of the spiritual practices of Hinduism, Buddhism, and Jainism. By cultivating mindfulness, one could become more aware of their inner state and to maintain a sense of calm and clarity. It was also seen as a way to reduce stress and anxiety, as well as to improve one's habits and behaviors. Ultimately, it was believed that by being mindful, one could become more aware of their connection to other living beings and the environment, and ultimately, to develop a sense of compassion and respect for all living things.

CHAPTER LXXXIII

The Nature of Enlightenment

The concept of enlightenment in ancient India was a crucial part of the spiritual and philosophical traditions of the subcontinent. The idea of enlightenment is an important concept in Hinduism, Buddhism, Jainism, and other religions that originated in India. Enlightenment can be seen as a state of spiritual awakening or expanded awareness, where an individual is no longer bound by the limitations of the physical world and is able to experience a greater sense of oneness with the universe. The concept of enlightenment was central to many of the ancient Indian spiritual traditions, with different schools of thought offering different interpretations of what it means to be enlightened.

In the Upanishads, a collection of ancient Hindu scriptures, enlightenment is seen as the realization of the true nature of the Self or Atman within each individual. According to the Upanishads, enlightenment is the experience of the Atman, which is seen as the eternal, unchanging essence of all existence. The Atman is seen as being beyond the physical form, and enlightenment is the realization that we are all connected to this eternal, divine source. When a person realizes this connection, they are said to be enlightened and liberated from the cycle of birth, death, and rebirth.

In Buddhism, enlightenment is seen as the experience of awakening to the truth of the Four Noble Truths. These truths state that all existence is characterized by suffering, that suffering has a cause, that suffering can be overcome, and that there is a path to freedom from suffering. Enlightenment is the experience of understanding these truths and the realization of the ultimate truth beyond the physical world. Enlightenment is also seen as the realization of the interconnectedness of all things, and the understanding that everything is empty of any separate existence.

In Jainism, enlightenment is seen as the realization of the inner truth of the soul. It is the experience of understanding that the soul is eternal, and that it is separate from the physical body and its attachments. Enlightenment is also seen as the experience of understanding that all existence is interconnected, and that we are all connected to the same source of divine energy.

The ancient Indian spiritual traditions all emphasize the importance of self-inquiry and spiritual practice as the means to enlightenment. Through meditation, contemplation, and other spiritual practices, individuals can begin to experience the higher truths that are beyond the physical world. The ultimate goal of these practices is to experience a state of oneness with the universe and to realize the ultimate truth that lies beyond the physical realm.

In conclusion, the concept of enlightenment in ancient India was an important part of the spiritual and philosophical traditions of the subcontinent. Different schools of thought offered different interpretations of what it means to be enlightened, but all emphasized the importance of spiritual practice and self-inquiry as the means to this ultimate experience. Enlightenment is seen as an experience of understanding the truth of the interconnectedness of all things, and the realization of the ultimate truth beyond the physical world.

CHAPTER LXXXIV

The Principles of Self-Realization

The ancient Indian civilization was built upon a foundation of understanding the metaphysical science of self-realization. This ancient wisdom was handed down from generation to generation, and the core teachings of self-realization have been passed down to us through the Vedic scriptures. Self-realization is the process of discovering the true nature of one's self, and it is the key to unlocking the mysteries of the universe.

The Vedic scriptures contain numerous teachings on the principles and practices of self-realization. These include the concept of Atman, which is the innermost self, as well as the concept of Brahman, which is the ultimate reality. The Vedic scriptures also teach the importance of discerning the truth and living in accordance with dharma, or one's rightful duty in life.

The practice of self-realization begins with an understanding of the three Gunas, or qualities of the soul, which are sattva, rajas, and tamas. Sattva is the quality of harmony and balance, rajas is the quality of action and energy, and tamas is the quality of darkness and inertia. By understanding and mastering these three qualities, one can attain a state of inner harmony and balance, which leads to a greater understanding of the true nature of reality.

The Vedic scriptures also emphasize the importance of meditation in self-realization. Meditation helps to still the mind and prepare it for the journey of self-discovery. Through meditation, one can achieve an awareness of the inner self and develop a sense of oneness with the cosmos.

The practice of yoga is also an important part of the process of self-realization. Through yoga, one can learn to control the body and mind and use them to focus on the higher levels of consciousness. Yoga helps to still the mind and open it up to the infinite potential of the universe.

The practice of bhakti yoga, or devotional service, is also essential to the process of self-realization. Bhakti yoga helps one to develop a personal relationship with the divine and to devote one's life to the service of the divine. Through bhakti yoga, one can experience a deep level of connection with the divine and a sense of oneness with all of creation.

Finally, the practice of Vedanta, or the inquiry into the ultimate reality, is also essential to the process of self-realization. Vedanta teaches that the ultimate truth is within oneself, and it is through the inquiry into the nature of reality that one can gain a deeper understanding of one's true self and the universe.

The principles of self-realization outlined in the Vedic scriptures have been followed for centuries in India, and they continue to be practiced today. Through the practices of meditation, yoga, bhakti yoga, and Vedanta, one can gain a deeper understanding of the true nature of reality and of one's own self. Self-realization is the key to unlocking the mysteries of the universe and to achieving inner peace and harmony.

CHAPTER LXXXV

The Art of Contemplation

The art of contemplation has been a part of Indian culture since ancient times. In the ancient Indian Sanskrit texts, contemplation was known as dhyana, which means "meditation" or "reflection". It is a practice of self-reflection in which one contemplates on their existence, their purpose in life, and their relationship to the world around them. The practice of contemplation has been used throughout the ages as a way to gain insight, clarity, and inner peace.

Contemplation is seen as an integral part of the spiritual traditions of India. It is thought to be the basis for self-realization and enlightenment. The Upanishads, which are ancient Indian philosophical texts, describe contemplation as the path to knowledge and self-realization. Ancient Hindu texts, such as the Bhagavad Gita, also emphasize the importance of contemplation in the pursuit of knowledge.

The practice of contemplation is deeply rooted in the Indian culture. It is connected with the practice of yoga and meditation, which are both considered essential elements of spiritual growth. In ancient India, contemplation was viewed as a way to transcend the mundane and to experience the divine. Contemplation was seen as a way to connect with the divine and to gain insight into the true nature of reality.

Contemplation was an important part of the spiritual practice of the Vedic period. During this period, the Vedic texts laid out the principles of contemplation and its importance in achieving spiritual liberation. It was believed that the practice of contemplation allowed one to gain access to the deeper levels of consciousness and to gain insight into the true nature of reality.

The practice of contemplation is still a part of the spiritual tradition of India. Today, many people still practice contemplation as a way to gain insight and inner peace. Contemplation is seen as a way to go beyond the mundane and to experience a higher state of consciousness. It is believed that through contemplation, one can gain a better understanding of their own nature and of the world around them.

The practice of contemplation has been an integral part of Indian culture for centuries. It is a way to gain insight, clarity, and inner peace. It is a practice that can lead to a greater understanding of the true nature of reality. The art of contemplation is an important part of the wisdom of lost Bharat and is still practiced today by many people.

CHAPTER LXXXVI

The Power of Intuition

The power of intuition is an ancient concept that has been practiced in India for thousands of years. Intuition has been seen as a divine, natural power that can be used to access knowledge and wisdom that is beyond the reach of the physical senses. In ancient India, intuition was seen as a way to gain insight into the true nature of reality.

In ancient India, intuition was not just seen as a way to access knowledge and wisdom, but also as a way to make decisions. Intuition was believed to be a powerful force that could guide people towards making the right choices in life. The ancient sages of India wrote extensively about the power of intuition and its importance in making decisions. They believed that intuition was an important source of information that could be used to make better decisions and avoid potential pitfalls.

The power of intuition was seen as a gift from the gods and was believed to be a part of each person's spiritual power. Intuition was seen as a divine force that could be accessed through meditation and other spiritual practices. The ancient sages of India taught that intuition was an important part of the spiritual path and could be used to gain insight into the true nature of reality.

The power of intuition was also seen as a way to access knowledge and wisdom that was not available through the physical senses. Intuition was seen as a source of divine knowledge that could be accessed through meditation and other spiritual practices. The ancient sages of India wrote extensively about the power of intuition and its importance in accessing knowledge and wisdom that was beyond the reach of the physical senses.

The power of intuition was also seen as a way to make decisions. The ancient sages of India wrote extensively about the power of intuition and its importance in making decisions. They believed that intuition was an important source of information that could be used to make better decisions and avoid potential pitfalls. The ancient sages of India taught that intuition was an important part of the spiritual path and could be used to gain insight into the true nature of reality.

The power of intuition was seen as a divine force that could be used to make wise decisions and access knowledge and wisdom that was not available through the physical senses. Intuition was seen as a powerful force that could be accessed through meditation and other spiritual practices. The ancient sages of India wrote extensively about the power of intuition and its importance in making decisions and accessing knowledge and wisdom that was beyond the reach of the physical senses.

The power of intuition was seen as a powerful force in ancient India and its importance was recognized by many of the ancient sages and spiritual teachers. Intuition was seen as a way to access knowledge and wisdom that was beyond the reach of the physical senses and was believed to be a part of each person's spiritual power. The ancient sages of India wrote extensively about the power of intuition and its importance in making decisions and accessing knowledge and wisdom that was beyond the reach of the physical senses.

The power of intuition was seen as a powerful force in ancient India and it is still seen as a powerful force today. Intuition is an important source of information that can be used to make better decisions and access knowledge and wisdom that is beyond the reach of the physical senses. Intuition is a powerful tool that can be used to gain insight into the true nature of reality and make wise decisions.

CHAPTER LXXXVII

The Practice of Spiritual Inquiry

The practice of spiritual inquiry is an ancient and powerful tradition found in India, known as Bharat. It is an ancient practice of contemplation and inquiry that is designed to lead one to a state of ultimate self-realization. It involves a deep exploration of one's innermost being, as well as an exploration of the greater universe and its laws.

At its core, spiritual inquiry is a search for understanding. It is a practice of questioning, learning, and growing in order to gain a greater insight into one's true nature and the nature of the universe. It is an exploration of the inner self and a journey of self-discovery, with the ultimate goal of achieving enlightenment.

The practice of spiritual inquiry in ancient India was rooted in the Vedic tradition. This tradition was based on the belief that the ultimate truth and knowledge could only be found within oneself. The Vedas, the most ancient of Hindu scriptures, contain numerous texts devoted to spiritual inquiry. These texts provide guidance on the path of spiritual inquiry, including instructions on meditation, contemplation, and concentration.

The practice of spiritual inquiry in ancient India was a process of self-transformation. It was a journey that required deep concentration, dedication and discipline. One had to be willing to open themselves to all forms of knowledge, in order to gain a greater understanding of the true nature of existence.

The practice of spiritual inquiry in ancient India was closely related to the practice spof yoga. Yoga was seen as a means of connecting to the divine and achieving inner peace. The practice of yoga provided a way to attain a higher level of consciousness and to experience a union with the divine.

The practice of spiritual inquiry in ancient India was also closely related to the practice of meditation. Meditation was seen as a way to focus the mind and to go beyond the physical body. It was believed that through meditation, one could access deeper levels of consciousness and gain greater insight into the true nature of reality.

The practice of spiritual inquiry in ancient India was also closely linked to the teachings of the Upanishads. The Upanishads are a collection of ancient texts that provide insight into the spiritual nature of reality. The Upanishads contain a number of ideas and teachings that can be used to explore the deeper aspects of life and to gain a greater understanding of the universe.

The practice of spiritual inquiry in ancient India was a process of self-discovery. It was a journey of contemplation and exploration that could lead one to a state of ultimate self-realization. Through this practice, one could gain a greater understanding of the true nature of existence and achieve a state of enlightenment.

The Wisdom of the Heart

The wisdom of the heart has been an integral part of Indian culture since ancient times. The ancient Indian sages and seers believed in the power of the heart to guide us in life, to help us make the right decisions, to understand the world around us, and to experience a deep sense of connection with the Divine. This wisdom of the heart has been passed down through generations in the form of stories, parables, and sayings.

In the ancient spiritual literature of India, the heart is often referred to as the source of all knowledge and insight. The Bhagavad Gita, for example, states that "the wise man should always be in the heart, for the heart is the source of all knowledge." This means that the heart is a repository of all knowledge and insight, and that it is from this source that we can gain a deeper understanding of the world and our place in it.

The ancient Indians believed that the heart was a portal to the divine, and that by connecting to it through meditation and contemplation, we can access the divine insight and wisdom that is essential for living a meaningful and fulfilling life. This connection to the divine is often referred to as "self-realization" or "enlightenment," and is seen as a path to achieving inner peace and harmony.

The wisdom of the heart is also a source of spiritual guidance, helping us see the divine in all things and to remain open to the possibility that life is full of mystery and wonder. According to the Upanishads, the ancient spiritual texts of India, "the heart is the gateway to wisdom, for in it lies the truth of all things." This means that by connecting to the wisdom of our hearts, we can open ourselves up to the possibility of experiencing a profound spiritual connection with the universe.

The wisdom of the heart is also a source of strength and courage. The Bhagavad Gita states that "the heart is the source of courage and strength, for the heart is the seat of all power." This means that by connecting to the wisdom of our hearts, we can access the courage and strength needed to take on life's challenges and to follow our dreams.

Finally, the wisdom of the heart is also a source of love and compassion. The Upanishads state that "the heart is the source of love, for in it lies the source of all kindness and compassion." This means that by connecting to the wisdom of our hearts, we can experience a deep sense of love and compassion for ourselves and for others.

The wisdom of the heart is an essential part of Indian culture, and has been passed down through generations of sages and seers. By connecting to the wisdom of our hearts, we can access the divine insight and guidance needed to live a meaningful and fulfilling life. By connecting to the wisdom of our hearts, we can also access the courage and strength needed to take on life's challenges, and to experience a deep sense of love and compassion for ourselves and for others. The wisdom of the heart is a source of power, insight, and spiritual guidance, and is essential for living a life of harmony and peace.

CHAPTER LXXXIX

The Nature of Love and Compassion

Love and compassion are ideals that have been revered in ancient India since time immemorial. Throughout the ages, these values have been passed down through the generations and continue to shape the culture of the country today.

In ancient India, love and compassion were seen as essential aspects of the human experience. They weren't simply an emotion, but rather a way of life. To the people of ancient India, love and compassion were seen as virtues that were essential for living a good life.

The ancient Indian scriptures, such as the Vedas and Upanishads, held love and compassion in high regard. The Bhagavad Gita, a sacred Hindu text, teaches us that love and compassion are essential in our relationships with others. It is said that love for one's fellow man is like a flame that can never be extinguished.

The ancient Indian sages and saints taught that love and compassion should be extended to all living beings, regardless of caste or creed. This is expressed in the Upanishads, which states that "all creatures are equal in the eyes of the Lord". This sentiment is echoed in the Bhagavad Gita, which states that "no one should be considered superior or inferior in this world".

In ancient India, love and compassion were also seen as a way to bring spiritual growth and enlightenment. It was believed that through love and compassion, one could attain inner peace and contentment. This is echoed in the teachings of the ancient Indian yogis, who taught that love and compassion are the keys to enlightenment.

The ancient Indian sages also taught that love and compassion should be practiced in all aspects of life. They taught that love and compassion should be extended to not just family, friends and acquaintances, but also to strangers. This is echoed in the teachings of the Bhagavad Gita, which states that "all creatures are to be loved equally".

All of these teachings of love and compassion were enshrined in the ancient Indian philosophical traditions, such as Vedanta and Samkhya. These traditions taught that love and compassion should be the guiding principles in all aspects of life. They also taught that through love and compassion, one could achieve spiritual liberation and enlightenment.

Love and compassion continue to be an integral part of Indian culture today. Throughout the country, these values are cherished and passed down from generation to generation. This is evidenced by the numerous festivals and celebrations which are centered around these values.

The nature of love and compassion in ancient India is reflected in its literature, art, and architecture. Examples of this can be seen in the many temples and monuments that were built in ancient India. These monuments were built not just to honor the gods, but also to celebrate the value of love and compassion.

The nature of love and compassion in ancient India is also reflected in its spiritual practices and beliefs. The ancient Indians believed that love and compassion were at the heart of the spiritual life. This is why they taught that all of the spiritual practices, such as yoga and meditation, should be guided by these values.

Love and compassion continue to be integral parts of the Indian culture today. These values have been passed down through the generations and continue to be celebrated in festivals and celebrations throughout the country. Through these values, the people of India have been able to maintain a sense of unity and harmony throughout the ages.

The Path of Surrender

The ancient Indian sages and mystics have long encouraged their followers to surrender to the will of God. This practice, known as prapatti or 'the path of surrender', is a fundamental tenet of Hinduism and is one of the oldest and most powerful spiritual paths in India. According to the teachings of the Vedas, we are all sparks of the divine and surrendering to the divine will brings us closer to the ultimate truth.

The concept of surrendering to God is deeply embedded in the Hindu scriptures and Upanishads. In the Bhagavad Gita, Lord Krishna encourages Arjuna to surrender to him, saying that he should give up all attachments and accept his own mortality. He further explains that by surrendering to the divine will, we can achieve inner peace and liberation.

Surrendering to the will of God is seen as a way of acknowledging and accepting the inescapable limitations of our existence. We often attempt to control our lives and the world around us, but ultimately all of our efforts are futile as we are powerless in the face of the divine will. By surrendering, we recognize our finite nature and accept our insignificance in the grand scheme of things.

The path of surrendering to God is also seen as a way of overcoming our egos. We often get caught up in our own desires and pursuits, and forget that our ultimate goal should be to serve God. By surrendering, we can detach ourselves from our own desires and accept the will of God. This allows us to develop a sense of humility and remove the veil of ego that obscures our spiritual path.

The practice of surrendering to God is seen as an essential part of spiritual growth and development. The great sages of ancient India have consistently encouraged their followers to surrender to the divine will. They emphasize that only by doing so can we truly progress on our spiritual journey.

Surrendering to God can also help us to overcome our fears and anxieties. When we surrender, we accept that whatever happens is in the hands of the divine. This can help us to detach ourselves from our own worries and fears and find inner peace.

The path of surrendering to God is an important part of ancient Indian spiritual practices. It allows us to overcome our ego, detach ourselves from our own desires and accept the will of the divine. By surrendering, we can achieve inner peace and serenity and make progress on our spiritual journey.

10. The Art of Wisdom

The Art of Wisdom is the practice of cultivating a deep understanding of oneself and the world around us. It involves a mastery of the power of reflection, the practice of discernment, and the nature of insight. The principles of righteousness, the art of living with integrity, and the power of self-knowledge are key components on the path of wisdom. Additionally, the practice of self-awareness and the wisdom of compassion are essential for spiritual growth and liberation.

The Power of Reflection

Reflection is the practice of taking time to think deeply and critically about one's experiences, beliefs, and values. Ancient India has long been known for its rich culture and spiritual practices. Reflection was a key part of the wisdom of lost Bharat. It was seen as a way to connect with the divine and gain insight into the true nature of reality.

The ancient Indians developed a variety of techniques to cultivate reflection. One of the most powerful was yoga. By uniting body, mind, and spirit, yoga allowed practitioners to explore the depths of their being and gain insight into life's mysteries. The practice of meditation was also a core part of reflection, as it allowed individuals to explore their own inner depths and gain a deeper understanding of themselves.

In addition to these practices, ancient Indian scholars developed sophisticated philosophical and literary works that encouraged reflection. The Upanishads, for example, are a collection of Hindu scripture that contain reflections on the nature of the universe and the soul. The Bhagavad Gita is another important text that contains reflections on the role of action and spiritual realization.

The practice of reflection was not just a personal pursuit. It was also used by the Indian leaders of the time. Kings and rulers would often consult with wise sages for advice and reflection on their decisions. This allowed them to gain a deeper understanding of their actions and their consequences.

Reflection was also seen as a way to cultivate wisdom. Ancient Indian thinkers believed that wisdom was not something that could be acquired through study and memorization, but rather it was something that could only be acquired through deep reflection and contemplation. In this way, reflection was seen as a powerful tool to gain insight into the true nature of reality.

The practice of reflection was also a part of the everyday lives of the people of ancient India. Every day, individuals would take time to reflect on their experiences and the world around them. This allowed them to gain a deeper understanding of the world and cultivate wisdom.

The power of reflection in ancient India was immense. It allowed individuals to gain insight into their own being and the universe around them. It also offered rulers and leaders a way to gain insight into their decisions and the consequences of their actions. Finally, it allowed everyone to cultivate wisdom and gain a deeper understanding of reality. In this way, reflection was an invaluable tool for the ancient Indians.

The Practice of Discernment

The practice of discernment was an important part of ancient Indian culture and was seen as a vital part of a person's spiritual development. Discernment was defined as the ability to differentiate between truth and falsehood, good and evil, and the beneficial from the harmful. It was believed that by developing this skill, one would become more discerning and wise in their decisions and actions.

Discernment was emphasized in many ancient Indian texts, including the Vedas, Upanishads, and the Bhagavad Gita. In the Bhagavad Gita, Krishna tells Arjuna that "a man of discernment acts only after due consideration." This statement is meant to emphasize the importance of considering all the facts before making a decision. It is also important to remember that discernment is not just about making decisions, but also about understanding the underlying meaning and purpose of those decisions.

In ancient India, the practice of discernment was closely related to the practice of yoga. Yoga is a spiritual practice that can help an individual to gain clarity, understanding, and wisdom. Through the practice of yoga, one can learn to observe their thoughts and feelings objectively and to gain a greater insight into their own motivations and desires. This helps them to make better decisions, as they are more aware of the consequences of their choices.

Another important practice in ancient India that encouraged the development of discernment was the practice of meditation. Meditation is a practice of stilling the mind and allowing the individual to become more aware of their innermost thoughts and feelings. Through this practice, one can gain insight into their true nature and develop the ability to discern between truth and falsehood.

The practice of discernment was also closely linked to the concept of dharma, which is the idea of living in accordance to one's dharma or purpose in life. Dharma emphasizes the importance of making decisions that are in harmony with one's true nature and the natural order of the universe. It is believed that through the practice of dharma, one can become more discerning and wise in their decisions and actions.

The practice of discernment was also closely linked to the concept of karma, which is the idea that one's present actions will determine their future experiences. Through the practice of karma, one can learn to make choices that will bring them closer to their true purpose and to their highest potential.

Finally, the practice of discernment was also closely linked to the practice of ahimsa, which is the practice of non-violence. Ahimsa teaches us to refrain from causing harm to any living being, including ourselves. Through this practice, one can learn to make decisions that will bring them closer to their highest potential and to their true purpose.

In conclusion, the practice of discernment was an important part of ancient Indian culture. It was seen as a vital part of a person's spiritual development and was closely linked to the practices of yoga, meditation, dharma, and ahimsa. Through the practice of discernment, one can become more discerning and wise in their decisions and actions, and can gain insight into their true nature and purpose.

CHAPTER XCIII

The Nature of Insight

In ancient India, insight was seen as a powerful tool for gaining knowledge and understanding. It was believed that insight could reveal truths that are hidden from the ordinary senses and even from reason. The Indian tradition of insight was based on the principles of yoga and meditation, and it was believed that insight could bring one closer to the ultimate truth.

Insight was seen as a way to gain knowledge and understanding of the world. It was believed that insight could provide answers to difficult questions, and it could illuminate the path to spiritual enlightenment. Insight was also seen as a way to bring harmony and balance to one's life. In the Indian tradition, insight was seen as a way to gain insight into the workings of the universe and to understand the true nature of reality.

The Indian tradition of insight also included the use of mantras and tantras. Mantras were believed to have great power, and they were used to bring about specific results. Tantras were used to guide and direct the energies of the practitioner in a specific direction.

Insight was also seen as a way to gain access to the hidden knowledge of the universe. Through insight, one could gain knowledge that would otherwise remain hidden from the ordinary senses. Insight was believed to be a powerful tool for understanding the workings of the universe and for achieving spiritual enlightenment.

Insight was also seen as a way to gain wisdom. It was believed that insight could provide answers to difficult questions and could help one to make wise decisions in life. Insight was also seen as a way to gain a better understanding of oneself and of the world around one.

In ancient India, insight was seen as a powerful tool for gaining knowledge and understanding. It was believed that insight could reveal truths that are hidden from the ordinary senses and even from reason. Through insight, one could gain access to the hidden knowledge of the universe and to achieve spiritual enlightenment. Insight was also seen as a way to gain wisdom and to make wise decisions in life. The Indian tradition of insight was based on the principles of yoga and meditation, and it was believed that insight could bring one closer to the ultimate truth.

The Principles of Righteousness

The ancient Indian culture is one of the oldest and most revered civilizations in the world. In India, the principles of righteousness have been highly valued since the ancient times. These principles have been enshrined in the various scriptures and teachings of the various Indian religious traditions. The ancient sages and seers of India have laid down a set of moral and ethical values, which have been accepted and respected by the Indian people for thousands of years. These principles of righteousness have been very important in guiding the Indian people in their everyday lives.

The most important of the principles of righteousness in ancient India were the four fundamental pillars of Dharma. These are known as the 'four legs of Dharma'. They are Ahimsa (non-violence), Satya (truthfulness), Asteya (not stealing) and Brahmacharya (celibacy). These four pillars of Dharma were the foundation of Indian civilization and the basis of morality in ancient India. These principles were strictly followed by all the rulers, citizens and members of the society.

Ahimsa, or non-violence, was the most important of the four principles. It was believed that all life is sacred and violence should be avoided at all costs. This principle was so deeply entrenched in Indian culture that even animals were protected from harm. It was also believed that one should never harm another human being. This principle of non-violence was so important that it was even adopted by the great Indian emperor, Ashoka, who made it one of the most important aspects of his policy.

Satya or truthfulness was another important principle of righteousness in ancient India. It was believed that one should always speak the truth and never lie. This principle was so important that even criminals were required to confess their crimes and tell the truth before they could be punished. Even in business transactions, it was required that both parties should tell the truth and not hide any important information.

Asteya, or not stealing, was another important principle of righteousness in ancient India. It was believed that one should never steal from another person or take something that does not belong to them. This principle was so important that even kings and rulers were expected to follow it.

The fourth pillar of Dharma was Brahmacharya, or celibacy. This is probably the most difficult of the four principles to follow, as it requires one to abstain from all sexual activity. It was believed that celibacy was essential for preserving one's spiritual purity and focusing on higher spiritual goals. This principle was so important that even the great sages of ancient India were expected to practice it.

The principles of righteousness in ancient India have been highly esteemed by the people of India for thousands of years. These principles continue to be the foundation of Indian culture and morality. They have been adopted by the various religions in India and continue to be one of the most important aspects of Indian society. The principles of righteousness have been enshrined in the various scriptures and teachings of the various Indian religious traditions and are still followed by many people today.

The Art of Living with Integrity

The concept of living with integrity in ancient India has been an integral part of the country's rich cultural heritage. It is believed that this kind of living was a major part of the way of life for the people of India for centuries. Living with integrity is about behaving in a manner that shows respect for oneself and for others. It is about being honest and truthful, and having the courage to stand up for what one believes in. In India, this concept of living with integrity was strongly embraced and it was believed that it was essential for a person to maintain their personal integrity in order to be successful in life.

In ancient India, the concept of living with integrity was closely linked to the spiritual belief system of the country. It was believed that by living an honest, truthful and compassionate life, one could achieve spiritual enlightenment and find true inner peace. The Indian scriptures, including the Upanishads, Bhagavad Gita, and the Vedas, all discuss the importance of living with integrity in order to achieve spiritual growth and enlightenment.

The concept of living with integrity in ancient India was also closely linked to the practice of Dharma, which is the spiritual law of the Universe. According to the Dharma, it is essential for individuals to lead a life of honesty and integrity in order to maintain their spiritual balance. A person's Dharma was believed to be their highest calling, and by living with integrity, it was believed that one could achieve spiritual enlightenment and harmony.

Another integral part of living with integrity in ancient India was the practice of Ahimsa, which is the concept of nonviolence. This concept was closely linked to the spiritual beliefs of the country and it was believed that by living a life of nonviolence and compassion, one could achieve spiritual enlightenment. Ahimsa was also believed to be the foundation of ethical behavior as it taught people to be tolerant, compassionate and understanding towards others.

The practice of living with integrity in ancient India was also closely linked to the practice of Karma. It was believed that Karma was a form of spiritual law, and that by living an honorable and truthful life, one could create positive Karma and avoid negative Karma. Karma was believed to be the cause of all actions, and it was believed that by living with integrity, one could create positive Karma and achieve spiritual enlightenment.

Overall, the concept of living with integrity in ancient India was an integral part of the country's spiritual and cultural heritage. It was believed that by living a life of honesty, truth, nonviolence and compassion, one could achieve spiritual growth and enlightenment. The practice of living with integrity was seen as a way to maintain one's spiritual balance, and by following these principles, one could create positive Karma and avoid negative Karma. This concept of living with integrity was highly respected and embraced by the people of ancient India, and it continues to be an important part of the country's spiritual and cultural heritage.

The Power of Self-Knowledge

The concept of self-knowledge has been a part of Indian culture since ancient times. It is believed that self-knowledge can lead to true happiness, inner peace and enlightenment. In the earliest texts of Indian philosophy, the Upanishads, the concept of self-knowledge is used to explain how individuals can achieve spiritual liberation. The Vedic tradition, which is the foundation of modern Hinduism, also emphasizes the importance of self-knowledge. The Bhagavad Gita, the most widely read scripture in India, teaches the power of self-knowledge in order to achieve spiritual enlightenment.

In ancient India, the power of self-knowledge was widely accepted as a way to reach an enlightened state of existence. According to the Upanishads, the highest truth is known only through self-knowledge. The Upanishads describe the power of self-knowledge as being able to reveal the innermost truth of one's being. This innermost truth is said to be the divine essence of the individual, or Atman. The Upanishads also state that self-knowledge is the only way to truly understand the nature of the universe and to realize one's true purpose in life.

The Bhagavad Gita is another ancient text that speaks of the power of self-knowledge. In this text, the power of self-knowledge is seen as a means of achieving spiritual liberation. The Bhagavad Gita teaches that self-knowledge is the key to understanding the true nature of reality. It states that by realizing one's true identity, one can gain a more profound understanding of the universe and its laws.

The concept of self-knowledge was also a part of the Vedic tradition. In the Vedas, self-knowledge was seen as the key to understanding the mysteries of the universe. Self-knowledge was believed to lead to spiritual liberation, inner peace and enlightenment. The Vedic tradition states that through self-knowledge, individuals can gain a deeper understanding of the true nature of reality and their place in it.

In ancient India, the power of self-knowledge was seen as an essential part of spiritual development. It was believed that by understanding one's true identity, an individual could gain a better understanding of the universe and its laws. Self-knowledge was also seen as a way to achieve inner peace and enlightenment. Through self-knowledge, individuals can gain a greater understanding of their place in the world and the ultimate purpose of their lives.

The concept of self-knowledge has been an integral part of Indian culture since ancient times. It is believed that by understanding one's true identity, an individual can gain a more profound understanding of the universe and its laws. Self-knowledge is seen as the key to spiritual liberation, inner peace and enlightenment. The power of self-knowledge is also seen as a way to achieve a higher state of consciousness, to understand the true nature of reality and to gain a better understanding of one's place in the world. Through self-knowledge, individuals can gain a better understanding of their purpose in life and achieve true happiness.

The Practice of Self-Awareness

The practice of self-awareness in ancient India has been an integral part of the wisdom of lost Bharat. Self-awareness or 'swadhyaya' in Sanskrit, has been mentioned in the Upanishads and other ancient Indian scriptures as a powerful tool for self-realization, transformation and liberation. In the Vedic tradition, self-awareness was seen as the highest form of spiritual practice that could lead to the ultimate goal of moksha or liberation.

Self-awareness is the practice of being mindful and aware of one's own thoughts, feelings, and behaviors. It is the process of observing oneself without judgment, and without attachment to any particular outcome. The practice of self-awareness is rooted in the Vedic teachings of mindfulness, which emphasize the importance of being aware of the present moment and not getting caught up in the stories of the past or the future.

In ancient India, self-awareness was seen as a way to reach deeper understanding of oneself and one's true nature. Through self-awareness, one can gain insight into the cause and effect of their actions, as well as the ways in which these actions manifest in their lives. The practice of self-awareness was seen as a powerful tool for personal transformation and liberation.

The practice of self-awareness was based on the idea that one must be aware of both the inner and outer world in order to make meaningful progress in life. By being mindful of one's thoughts, feelings, and behaviors, one can gain a better understanding of the dynamics of the world around them. This allows them to make decisions that are grounded in wisdom, rather than in fear or ignorance.

In the Vedic tradition, self-awareness was seen as a way of cultivating sattva or purity of mind. Through self-awareness, one can observe and become aware of their own thoughts and feelings, as well as the thoughts and feelings of others. This helps to cultivate a sense of balance and clarity, and to remain grounded in the present moment.

The practice of self-awareness in ancient India was also seen as a way to develop compassion and empathy. Through self-awareness, one can become aware of the suffering of others, and can develop an understanding of how their actions can affect others. This allows one to become aware of their own actions and how they can be used to help or harm those around them.

The practice of self-awareness in ancient India was seen as a powerful tool for personal transformation and liberation. By becoming aware of one's thoughts, feelings, and behaviors, one can gain insight into their own inner world, and can use this insight to make meaningful changes in their life. This can lead to greater fulfillment, contentment, and peace.

The Wisdom of Compassion

The ancient Indian culture was one that was steeped in wisdom and compassion, a strength of character that has been passed down through generations. The idea of compassion is one that has been deeply embedded in the Indian culture for centuries. It is something that is both held in great reverence and respected as a way of life.

The history of India is filled with stories of compassion and understanding, from the tales of the Mahabharata to the teachings of the Upanishads. In the Mahabharata, for example, the Pandavas are shown to be compassionate even in the face of adversity, showing their understanding of what is just, even in the midst of war. This is a reflection of the importance of compassion in Indian culture.

Compassion is also an integral part of Hinduism and Buddhism, two of the most popular religions in India. Hinduism teaches that it is important to be compassionate towards all living beings and to show mercy even in difficult situations. Buddhism, meanwhile, encourages people to cultivate compassion and to use it to help others. Both religions emphasize the importance of being compassionate, even in difficult situations, and of helping those less fortunate.

One of the most influential figures in Indian history, Mahatma Gandhi, was a firm believer in the power of compassion. He argued that it was an essential part of a person's character and that it should be displayed in all areas of life. He encouraged people to be kind to one another and to show compassion even to those who were different from them. He believed that it was a great power and that it could help to create a more peaceful and just society.

Compassion is also a part of many of the traditional Indian values, such as ahimsa (non-violence) and satyagraha (peaceful protest). Ahimsa is the belief that all living beings, regardless of their species, should be treated equally and with respect. This includes animals, plants, and even inanimate objects. Satyagraha is the belief that peaceful protest is the best way to achieve justice and that violence should not be used to achieve one's goals. Both of these values emphasize the importance of compassion and understanding in order to create a more peaceful world.

The wisdom of compassion in ancient India is something that is still relevant today. It teaches us to be kind and understanding to all living beings, to look beyond our own interests, and to recognize the suffering of those around us. It is a reminder of the importance of being compassionate, even in difficult situations, and it encourages us to use our compassion to try to create a more just and peaceful world. Compassion is a powerful force and it is something that we can all strive to embody.

The Nature of Spiritual Growth

The spiritual growth of individuals in ancient India was rooted in the Vedic tradition. This spiritual growth was focused on the attainment of moksha, or liberation from the cycle of birth and death. The Vedas, the oldest Hindu scriptures, contain many passages that describe the spiritual journey and its various stages. This path to spiritual growth was based on the concept of karma, or the law of cause and effect. According to this law, one's current situation is a result of one's past actions, and one's future will be determined by one's current actions.

The Vedas describe a four-fold path to moksha, or spiritual growth. This path consists of karma yoga, jnana yoga, bhakti yoga, and raja yoga. Karma yoga is the path of action, where one performs deeds in accordance with dharma (righteousness) and works to develop detachment from the results. Jnana yoga is the path of knowledge, where one explores the nature of the self and the universe and strives for the realization of oneness with the divine. Bhakti yoga is the path of devotion, where one develops a loving, personal relationship with the divine and practices an attitude of surrender. Finally, raja yoga is the path of meditation, where one practices breath control and concentration to still the mind and cultivate inner peace.

The Vedic tradition also emphasizes the importance of purifying one's mind and body in order to achieve spiritual growth. This was achieved through practices such as fasting and purification rituals, which helped to cleanse the body and mind of negative energies and prepare the individual for spiritual growth. Additionally, the Vedic tradition placed a great emphasis on spiritual study and contemplation. Through study and contemplation, one could gain knowledge and insight into the nature of the self and the divine, and cultivate the qualities of wisdom, compassion, and love.

The spiritual growth of individuals in ancient India was further augmented by the practice of yoga. Yoga is an ancient practice that seeks to unite the body, mind, and spirit. Through yoga, individuals can cultivate mental, physical, and spiritual health and well-being. Yoga promotes the development of physical strength, flexibility, balance, and coordination. It also helps to cultivate mental clarity and awareness, and to cultivate the qualities of love, compassion, and patience. Additionally, yoga helps to cultivate a sense of connectedness with the divine, which enhances the individual's spiritual growth.

The Nature of Spiritual Growth in ancient India was rooted in the Vedic tradition. This spiritual growth was focused on the attainment of moksha, or liberation from the cycle of birth and death. The Vedas, the oldest Hindu scriptures, contain many passages that describe the spiritual journey and its various stages. This path to spiritual growth was based on the concept of karma, or the law of cause and effect. Additionally, the Vedic tradition emphasized the importance of purifying one's mind and body in order to achieve spiritual growth through practices such as fasting and purification rituals. Finally, the practice of yoga helps to cultivate mental, physical, and spiritual health and well-being, as well as a sense of connectedness with the divine, which enhances the individual's spiritual growth. By following this path, individuals in ancient India were able to achieve spiritual growth and attain moksha, or liberation from the cycle of birth and death.

CHAPTER C

The Path of Liberation

The path of liberation in ancient India was a spiritual journey that was sought by many to achieve inner peace and enlightenment. It was a complex concept that was deeply rooted in the culture and traditions of the region. The path of liberation was a way to free oneself from the bondage of worldly desires and attachments, and to reach a higher level of understanding and awareness. The belief was that the individual can transcend the material world and reach a state of perfect contentment, peace and joy.

In ancient India, the path of liberation was often referred to as moksha, which is derived from the Sanskrit word meaning "release" or "freedom." Moksha was seen as the ultimate goal of life and the end of the cycle of rebirth. It was a journey of personal transformation and spiritual growth. There were various paths that could be taken to reach moksha, and one of the most popular paths was yoga.

Yoga was an ancient Indian system of physical, mental, and spiritual practices that aimed to unify the individual with the divine. It was a practice of self-discipline and meditation that was believed to lead to inner peace and enlightenment. The practice of yoga included postures (asanas), breathing exercises (pranayama), and mindfulness and concentration (dhyana). The goal of yoga was to quiet the mind and bring the individual closer to the divine.

Another path of liberation that was popular in ancient India was Jainism. Jainism is an ancient religion that emphasizes non-violence and the spiritual liberation of all living beings. Jains believe in reincarnation and the liberation of the soul from the cycle of suffering and death. They also believe that one must practice right knowledge, right faith, and right conduct in order to reach moksha.

The path of liberation in ancient India was also known as the path of knowledge. It was believed that knowledge was the key to unlocking the mysteries of life and to achieving a higher level of spiritual understanding. The Upanishads, ancient Hindu texts, taught the path of knowledge which consisted of the four Vedas. These Vedas, which are composed of hymns, mantras, and rituals, were seen as a source of spiritual knowledge.

The path of liberation in ancient India was also known as the path of devotion. It was believed that one could reach moksha by dedicating themselves to the divine and cultivating an attitude of love and devotion. Devotion was seen as an essential part of the spiritual path and was often expressed through prayer, worship, and rituals.

The path of liberation in ancient India was a long and arduous journey that required dedication and discipline. It was a spiritual journey that was meant to bring the individual closer to the divine and to reach a state of perfect contentment, peace and joy. Although the path of liberation was difficult, it was seen as a necessary step for those seeking inner peace and enlightenment.